I would like to dedicate this book to my new grandson
Michael Caleb Bivona Gharib, born October 1, 2010,
to my daughter Laurie and son-in-law Clint.

Was That Me?

Turning Points in My Life by Mike Bivona

Michael Bivona

Order this book online at www.trafford.com
or email orders@trafford.com

Most Trafford titles are also available at major online book retailers.

Printed in the United States of America.

ISBN: 978-1-4269-3755-2 (sc)
ISBN: 978-1-4269-3756-9 (hc)
ISBN: 978-1-4269-3757-6 (e)

Library of Congress Control Number: 2010912416

*Our mission is to efficiently provide the world's finest, most comprehensive book publishing
service, enabling every author to experience success. To find out how to publish your book,
your way, and have it available worldwide, visit us online at www.trafford.com*

Trafford rev. 10/07/2010

 www.trafford.com

North America & international
toll-free: 1 888 232 4444 (USA & Canada)
phone: 250 383 6864 ♦ fax: 812 355 4082

Contents

Acknowledgements

I would like to give special thanks to my soul mate Barbara Bivona for her patience and understanding while I secluded myself writing this and my other books. I would also like to thank her for the endless hours she spent acting as my sounding board, advisor, proofreader, and for her gentle constructive criticism.

My special thanks to my sister Anne who rose to the occasion after my mother Margaret Concetta passed away in 1947 at age 47. She unselfishly took over the responsibilities of managing our household and caring for my father Luciano, my sister Mae, and me.

My father and his second wife Mary DiAngelo were also very supportive while I attended college and made sure that there was a place for me to live, study and dine.

I thank my brother Vic and his wife Rose whose encouragement and good cooking helped me through my years studying at Long Island University.

The many friends that I met along the way that willingly guided me over some pretty rough terrain deserve special thanks. Police officer Maloney, thank you for not putting me in detention; instead of harsh punishment, he took me by the ear and led me home, and was responsible for my joining the PAL (Police Athletic League) at a time in my life that I was naive and vulnerable. His friendship certainly made a difference in the direction that I would travel for the rest of my life.

My commanding officer in the United States Air Force, Major Johnson, who saw that I had potential, which I was not aware of, and encouraged me to better myself. I owe him a debt of gratitude for his guidance and insistence that I complete my high school education before I left the military.

I have to thank the many friends that I met while attending college for their help with my initial courses at the university. Without their understanding and guidance, I certainly would have not successfully completed my studies and graduated.

Lastly I would like to thank the many professors at Long Island University who were my mentors and eventually my friends. Special thanks to Professor Emeritus Philip Wolitzer, former Dean of the Accounting Department and Professor Joseph Friedman of the English Department, for taking an interest in my future and for their encouragement and good will, especially when I had doubts about my progress.

Chapter One – Developing My Character

In early 2008, I came across a unique website, "The East New York Project," WWW.tapeshare.com., which included interesting information about the Brooklyn, New York neighborhood I grew up in. The site was developed by Riccardo (Rick) Gomes who spent his informative years in that section of Brooklyn. The site includes lots of history and renderings of before-and-after photos of movie theaters, playgrounds, street activity, and many buildings as they appeared in earlier-times and at present. An interesting segment is the presentation of people in sections of East New York, and the years the photos were taken, with brief descriptions of the participants, and the occasions that resulted in taking the pictures. When I first visited the incredible site it was in its infancy (began in 2005). It is now overflowing with information and links to other sites. It is incomprehensible how Rick manages the influx of data that seems to keep pouring in from former residents and other interested parties. He certainly is a busy guy and a testament to what amazing things can be accomplished if you are passionate and love what you're doing.

I contacted Rick and asked what made him take on such an enormous undertaking? He responded that "I never thought that the site would draw so much attention and such a voluminous amount of data." He emailed me that the concept for the genesis of the site is in two parts:

"The human part – My brothers and I wanted to try to bring back something we had lost; the disintegration of the neighborhood and its memories. We grew up in a multi-generational environment and fled to the suburbs, which separated us from our friends and the intimacy of close-knit families. My mother had a passion for taking pictures of her family and friends in the Brooklyn neighborhood. Going through her photo albums made me think that there had to be plenty of people who had taken pictures of their friends and neighborhoods, and if we could put them together into one large virtual album, we could recreate some precious memories and historical data for posterity. We didn't know if it would reach a critical enough mass that would help bring old friends back together, but certainly understood the possibilities.

The technical side – The inspiration came from a site called 'My Brooklyn.' It is a running log of comments in text only. One night my brothers and I took our parents out for their anniversary and decided to construct a post on that site. We started brainstorming about how much better the site would be with images, history, chat-rooms, etc. Believe it or not, my brother wanted to do it for all of Brooklyn. He had been collecting postcards from EBay and thought that having 'before and after' images using 'morphing' software to show a street changing over time would be a fun endeavor. I designed a prototype and quickly came to the conclusion that we had better limit the effort to our childhood neighborhood of East New York. Once I worked out my design, I set it up and sort of leaked out what we were trying to do. I had a short mailing list culled from several internet bulletin boards, but mostly wanted our project spread by word-of-mouth. If we received a positive reaction and got people to send pictures, I would stick with the site and continue its growth. That was in 2005. We have had a steady stream of positive feedback and contributions of stories and images ever since. Yes, it does consume a lot of my time, but it is a 'Labor of love' like any good hobby should be."

A copy of page 1 of the "East New York Project" follows with Rick's permission:

| • Home | • Zone 1 | • Zone 2 | • Zone 3 | • Zone 4 | • Zone 5 | • Zone 6 | • Highld Park |

About the East New York Project

The East New York Project is a multimedia archive of the history of my childhood neighborhood. In general, it is the area currently referred to as the Highland Park area in Brooklyn, bordered by Atlantic Avenue to the south, Elderts Lane to the East, and Broadway to the West. However we also feature pictures and history south of Atlantic as well. It is intended to be a collaborative effort, and contributions in the form of stories, pictures, and even video are welcome. Use the menu bar above to navigate to areas of interest.

The Brian Merlis images have arrived!

We have joined with noted Brooklyn collector and author Brian Merlis to bring some spectacular images to the East New York Project. Those interested in more images and a list of Brian's books should visit his site Old Brooklyn Pix

St. Rita's Class of 1960 Reunion Alert!

Charles Passentino is arranging a reunion in the spring for classes 8-A and 8-B, 1960. Please contact him at bklyneagle@aol.com if you are interested.

What's New

*************************Special Request******************************
I've been approached by The National League of POW/MIA Families looking for information on a Richard Joseph Russano. He went MIA in Vietnam in 1970. Richard's family lived on Elderts Lane and he may have attended ENY Vocational High School in the late 1960s. If you were a classmate of his drop me a line at tapeshare@yahoo.com, we are trying to identify a school and possible graduation year.
****

I wasn't ready to post an update, but the Norwood Palace made the news when police shot and killed a security guard who was working there on Sunday night. I've chosen to offset that bit of bad news with some historical trivia about Norwood Avenue courtesy of Gerry Carter. He reminded me that Tommy Gallagher, who won the 1959 147 lb novice class Golden Gloves title, lived a few houses away from him on Jamaica off Norwood. Tommy also starred as the trainer in the TV reality series, The Contender. Gerry had the Daily News archives post up a photo from the fight which I am posting temporarily as a plug for their photo archives.

Nov 2 - This one is not a trivia question. I was tempted to title this update "A Funny Thing Happened on the way to the Muni Archives". While researching other locations on microfilm I stumbled on some interesting things and this magnificent house used to sit on Pennsylvania Avenue. It was built for a lawyer before 1910, and was occupied by another lawyer in 1930. That small octagonal building to the left is still standing. For other tax photo gems, I added the little-known Sheridan Theater and a house that appeared to have a graveyard for a front lawn on the Liberty Avenue page in Zone 6. On the Wyona Street page (Zone 1) there is

The horizontal bar includes a Home page and Zones 1-6 plus the Highland Park area of East New York. The Home page is extensive and includes an alphabetical Directory of contributors to the project, an index of images of places of worship, public schools, recreation venues and other places of interest, such as: links to related sites, neighborhood reunions, mystery photos and related contacts. All the images and information are a click away from the viewing screen. The zones include many of the streets in various sections of East New York, with pictures of before-and-after images of places and people, with descriptions and background stories that keep the reader transfixed on its pages, absorbing the history and familiarity of the faces and places. Rick's time and patience certainly resulted in an extremely sophisticated and a technologically advanced website that he miraculously continues to maintain.

So what does all of this have to do with the turning-points in my life that eventually led to the person that I am today? Well, I was so fascinated with the project that I decided to add a few of my over fifty-year-old pictures to the embroidery. The picture below of "My Gang," which appears in Zone 5, caught the attention of one of my teenage buddies, Rod Maggio. He recognized the guy on the left making a muscle as "moi." On my left are Tony (Tough Guy) Galucci, Tony (Big Salute) Sturiano, and Pete (Ears) Basile. The bottom row is Pete (The Face) Sturiano, Louie (Knuckles) Skita and his brother Mike (The Arm) Skita. The guy on top is Leo (Shorty). I don't remember his last name, but he was the toughest guy in the neighborhood. Due to the mop of red wavy hair my moniker was . . . Red.

Rod Maggio contacted me and after a few weeks of bantering back and forth and catching up on where our old-time friends were, he asked the question that got me thinking about the events that led to my present existence. He said, "The last time we spoke (over fifty years ago) you decided to find a job and skip high school. How did you go from never attending high school to becoming a college graduate, CPA, author, historian, philanthropist and recipient of the '2007 Distinguished Alumni Achievement Award' from Long Island University?" I asked him where he attained all the information about me, and he said, "Simple, I put your name in my computer search engine and with a little patience accumulated a mini-bio."

The question haunted me for some time as my children also asked me the same question over the years and never received a rational explanation from me. My answer was always a quick response that included, lots of luck, fate, or it was my destiny. I never really thought about the events and turning-points that led me from a jagged past to the smooth plateau that became my adult life. We all ask ourselves, from time to time, how we arrived at a particular place in our lives? The answers are usually attributed to specific events that caused us to be where we are. We rarely delve into the reasons or circumstances that caused us to reach our current destination. Were the reasons destiny? Luck? Being at the right place at the right time? Our environment? Our friends? Or was it our temperament or character that led us to our present place? The answer is probably a little of each. In my case, when looking back I've asked myself: how did I go from never attending high school to becoming a college graduate, Certified Public Accountant and an author of three books? Looking back to my formative years, I often wondered if the person of my teens was really me.

There is no doubt that a person's temperament plays a key role in decisions that are made and leads one to their place in life. I would like to revisit my children's question, "How did you zigzag through life and get to be the person you are today?" To be specific, I never really gave much thought to the details; I just went with the flow and enjoyed the ride. But for my own edification I will try to pinpoint explicit events that guided me along the way.

It is easy to recognize that a person's temperament is the critical guiding point in one's life, but what leads a person to have a particular temperament? Are genetics, environment, experience, schooling, a person's appearance or just luck responsible for the building blocks that result in one's character? In my experience in the computer industry, I would give employees the same opportunity to advance themselves in the company by their solving specific business problems that had only one answer. Invariably I would get different solutions to the same problems, in many instances employees wouldn't even attempt to participate in an effort that could advance them in the organization. Why do people who are faced with the same situations end up making different decisions and choosing different paths? Why then, when windows of opportunity arise, do people that are given the same chance, choose to take different roads? There is no one answer to this question, but I think by examining my past I might find some rational reasons that led me to becoming the person I am today.

One of the earliest influences in my life that was probably the first link in a long character-building-chain was that my father, Luciano Joseph Bivona, who was from a small town in Sicily by the name of Bivona, decided to change his religion from Catholic to Seventh Day Adventist. This happened a year before I was born in 1934, when we lived at 681 Liberty Avenue in the East New York section of Brooklyn. It was, to say the least, a very busy two-way street with a predominant population of Italian speaking immigrants and their American born children. A photo of the heavily trafficked street follows:

There was so much traffic that my older sister Mae (Rosaria), who was named after my mother's mother, was run down by a car at age five and had to be rushed to Unity hospital with a fractured skull. Our apartment building was next to a barber shop in a three-family house. My mother's friend, Jenny DeNino, her husband Rocco and their son and three daughters lived on the first floor. The landlord, Anile (Arnie the barber) Russo, his wife Lily and their five children lived on the second floor and the Bivonas and their four children lived on the third floor. Arnie had a barber shop on the ground floor next door to us, which is where I had my first hair trimming at age four. I didn't appreciate the event and remember screaming and kicking until a lollypop appeared and miraculously calmed me down. His wife Angie ran an Italian style deli on the right of the barber shop so the air was always perfumed with the smell of provolone cheese, olives and a mix of other exotic odors. Our home is to the left of the trolley car in the photo, which passed by quite often, making loud bone-chilling-clanking sounds in the process. We also had a firehouse on the next street which was quite active, the fire trucks made frequent trips in and out of the station blowing their horns and blasting sirens to clear the paths to their destinations. The noise level on the block was quite high, but after living within its confines for many years, we got used to the high decibels.

My father, at age 12, came to the United States from the small Town of Bivona in Sicily, Italy. He crossed the Atlantic Ocean with his mother Angelina Bivona on an immigration ship to join his father Victor in the East New York Section of Brooklyn. I could picture my grandfather Victor and his brother, my great-uncle Joe, waiting for them at the docks in New York City. My father was from a long line of Catholics, and shocked everyone when he had a new religious calling and decided to become a Seventh Day Adventist, much to the chagrin of my mother, Margaret (Concetta), and the rest of our family and friends. So I was born into that Protestant religion and was raised in an atmosphere of strict Bible reading, prayer, going to church on Saturday (Sabbath), and adherence to the Ten Commandments. It immediately made me an outsider in my neighborhood, as other children my age were mostly Italian-Catholics. One of my most difficult adjustments was that we attended church on Saturday and all my friends' families were Sunday worshipers. Walking to the subway on the Sabbath dressed in my "Sunday best," resulted in all sorts of wisecrack remarks from my neighborhood buddies, which invariably ended up with me fighting with many of them when my father wasn't around. So, as time went by, my skin got tough defending myself from outside adversity, and my heart got soft from my religious upbringing, especially the "Turning the other cheek" part. An interesting event took place when I was about one-year-old. My grandmother, Angelina, who was a devout Catholic, decided to baby-sit with me. My parents gladly took the invitation and turned me over to her loving arms. She didn't waste any time getting me to St. Michael's Church on Liberty Avenue to have me baptized in the Catholic religion, therefore guaranteeing that my chances of going to heaven were greatly improved. As the story goes, my father was livid that his mother would do such a thing without his permission. Her answer was quite firm, she said: "You can do with your life as you please, but your son's life is my business."

When I was five years old, we moved further down the avenue to 545 Liberty Avenue, again next to a storefront, this time in a two-family house owned by the Bono family. The street wasn't as busy as my birth-home, but there was enough traffic for me to get hit by a car and rushed to Unity hospital at the tender age of five; something my sister Mae and I had in common. We were both hit by cars on Liberty Avenue, when we were five-years-old, both sustaining fractured skulls. I spent over a month in the hospital recovering from my fracture. I was treated so well by the nurses that I thought I was on a special holiday vacation. They patted and rubbed my curly-red-hair so often that I thought my red hair had mystical powers, as a treat of sorts always followed the ritual.

A favorite game that my friends and I played was hitching rides on the back of trolley cars that passed frequently on our street. Some of the older boys thought it was fun to wrap the trolley's cable line around a ring at the rear of the car which caused it to lose contact with the overhead electric power source; this caused the cable to disconnect resulting in the trolley screeching to a halt, much to the dismay of the passengers and driver. The boys would laugh themselves silly watching the car operator trying to untangle the lines. Luckily I was too young to take part in that dangerous game. Needless to say that after two near fatal accidents on that busy avenue, and the possibility that more of the same was forthcoming, my parents decided to move to a safer location in a residential neighborhood.

Fortunately we moved to a less dangerous part of East New York, 589 Cleveland Street on the corner of Blake Avenue, where the neighborhood had a mixture of Catholics, Protestants and thank God, many Jews. The reason I say, "Thank God, many Jews" is because that is where I learned to make money by being of service to others. On the Sabbath, the little redheaded "Goy" was their favorite, if not the only one, willing to perform many of the chores that were restricted on the Sabbath in the Jewish religion on their day of rest, such as lighting candles and gas stoves. Of course I did this without my father's knowledge, as his new religion had the same prohibitions as the Jewish faith. On Blake Avenue there was a Jewish pushcart market with street vendors lined up for several blocks. I was also a favorite of theirs for tending carts when the owners wanted a break, and was able to add a few shekels to my pockets while learning some serious business practices on getting along with customers and people from different ethnic backgrounds. The experience certainly was a character-builder and was, without-a-doubt, responsible for most of my future partners in business being Jewish. In my accounting practice our firm's name was, Bivona, Ambrico & Dlugacz, Certified Public Accountants. In my computer business, Manchester Technologies, Inc., my partners' last names were Steinberg and Stemple and in some of my real estate partnerships my partners' last names were, Kressel and Rothlein. As a matter of fact, my most important lifelong partner is my beautiful Jewish wife Barbara Selden. Blake Avenue became an important part of my growing up experience. When I was 15 years old, my friend Frank Curti (my future brother-in-law's brother) and I decided to go into business together on that busy avenue. I had a brainstorm; I thought that since the neighborhood had a large population of African-Americans, it would be a good idea to set up a stand during the Christmas holidays and sell dolls that would appeal to that population. So we bought over 200 beautiful brown dolls of various sizes, from 12-inches to 36-inches and displayed them alongside their Caucasian sisters. Well, our first business venture was an absolute failure, we sold all 100 of our white dolls but very few of the dark ones. It seemed that everyone preferred the light skinned, blonde haired ones, including our

African-American customers. We eventually sold most of them at below cost, which resulted in a loss for us. Our nieces received the remnants of our unsold stock under their Xmas trees that year, which they were delighted with. It was another lesson learned and a link added to my growing character-chain; there are no guarantees in business, regardless of how promising the prospects, and most certainly regardless of how rational the venture may seem.

We only lived on Cleveland Street for a few years, but they were some of the most memorable and influential in my childhood. I made many friends of different ethnic backgrounds who I'm still in touch with today. While living there WWII broke out and my big brother Vic joined the United States Marines to help shorten the war. I was only eight years old and his leaving was a traumatic experience for me. He was my role model and the thought of never seeing him again was frightening. Another unwelcomed event at the same age was a second fractured skull that I received while playing with my friends at the New Lots Avenue Park. My friend Jimmy pushed me from the top of a slide and I went down head first. Straight to the hospital for another month long special holiday vacation. This experience was a little more serious, but I still got my head-rubs and plenty of hugs and kisses followed by presents from the ever affectionate and concerned nurses. Of course my parents were beside themselves and didn't know what to do with the red-headed rascal that kept getting into all sorts of mischief, some of which was life-threatening. This mishap caused me to miss many of my classes in elementary school, which resulted in my not advancing to the next grade with my friends. Initially when teachers and friends spoke of my being left behind other students it was always because I spent most of the term in the hospital and at home recuperating. But in time, the reason for not advancing vanished and the only statement I heard was "He was left behind." The stigma stayed with me and was probably one of the reasons that I disliked going to school and played hooky as often as I could, resulting in my avoiding junior high school. In time my parents decided to move again, it was my fourth move in ten-years, I was beginning to think that we were gypsies!!

At age ten the links in my character-chain were rapidly connecting. We moved to another section of East New York; 2244 Pitkin Avenue, between Van Siclen and Hendrix Streets. There are no available photos of the location at the time we moved there, but I was able to get a current photo, which by the way, shows a great improvement from the beat-up premises that we lived in. As a matter of fact, the whole neighborhood has been recycled and is a vast improvement from when we lived there over 50 years ago. In the photo below there are new houses on Hendrix Street that replaced the older run-down ones. My building was evidently renovated by the "99 Cents Express Store," and resembles a healthy business with livable space above. The parking lot on the right was a wire factory with large spools of wire sitting in an open area. My bedroom was over the still unsightly door (it's probably the same door I used). The photo of my former residence was taken by my friend Rod Maggio, who lived only a few blocks away, and is presented with his permission:

There was an elevator train running outside my bedroom which rocked me to sleep every night; a corner supermarket below our second floor apartment (there was one other apartment above us), and the Lyric movie theatre directly across the street. To the left of our apartment was the Van Siclen Avenue train station, Brant's Ice Cream Parlor, a dry cleaning store and a Jewish delicatessen. Across the street was a saloon (drinking establishment), two candy stores (one with an eating area and a sit down counter), a Chinese laundry and a shoemaker. The neighborhood had the same ethnic mix as Cleveland Street except that there were African-Americans living on the same block across the street over the larger candy store. Talk about a melting pot; with few exceptions we all got along very well, especially when playing stickball and punchball. Needless to say, my two older sisters, Anne (the oldest) and Mae (Rosaria) joined me in a state-of-shock at living in such a busy, run-down neighborhood. But transportation to work was nearby for my father and my mother's friend, Jenny DeNino, who also lived in the same building that I was born in on Liberty Avenue, lived above us in our latest home. So there we were, my sister Anne at age 16, Mae at 14 and me at age 10 going to new schools and making new friends in a not so friendly neighborhood. My brother Victor was in the Marine Corps and fighting in the Pacific during WWII, so he was spared the experience of being the "New guy" on the block. At first I had to fight my way to school because I was the only Christian anyone ever met who went to church on Saturday, but fortunately I was a good stickball and punchball player, so I eventually became one of the "boys," and the fighting was less frequent.

I spent my informative years, from 10 to 18, in that shabby neighborhood, spending a great deal of time on the streets playing ball, drinking cokes and listening to music from the juke boxes in the candy stores and ice cream parlor, while becoming friendly with the local girls, and occasionally having fights with gangs from other neighborhoods. A major event on the block was shooting craps (dice) on the street corners or in available empty hallways. As a teenager I spent most of my spare time at Larry's

Pool Hall, just two blocks from my house. The hall is where the older guys in the neighborhood hung out and where I was to learn to be "Seen and not heard." The older guys required absolute silence so they could focus on playing that very competitive game. Although I never mastered the game, it was here that I learned that "Practice makes perfect," as the champion players would practice for endless hours each day honing their skills in anticipation of winning lots of money from their competitors when playing straight pool, eight-ball, nine-ball and money- ball. Another lesson I learned in the pool hall was that when it comes to talent, there is always someone, at some-point-in- time that is going to empty your pockets by beating you at your own game. All of these experiences were adding links to my character-chain, and slowly forming my personality.

The most tragic event of my life was when my mother Margaret Concetta died at age 47, when I was 13 years old. My sister Anne, who was married at the time and had a son of her own, (my nephew Dennis J. Pierce), took over the household chores, which included caring for me, my sister Mae and my father; she did this while holding down a part-time job.

I was attending Junior High School 149 at the time, which was on Sutter and Miller Avenues. It was a short six block walk from my house, which made the journey tolerable for me as I was losing interest in school and playing lots of hooky. The times I attended school I enjoyed playing punchball in the school-yard and typing. Why typing? Well there was a beautiful young teacher with what I considered at that time the most beautifully endowed breasts that drew me to her class like a magnet. The class was elective, so I was the only boy in the class and took lots of ribbing from my buddies, until they peeked into the classroom and saw my purpose in life. To please Miss Baily, I became the best typist in the class, always cherishing the praise and attention she bestowed on me. One of my rewards was her patting me on my enormous flock of curly-red-hair, which always got me to blush with an equally enormous smile. As strange as it may seem, being able to type well became very instrumental in my journey through manhood and business, especially when computers became available to the general public and most men didn't know how to handle a keyboard.

Some of my most memorable experiences were on the baseball field playing with the Police Athletic League's (PAL) baseball division. The organization was established in 1914 in New York City. It has provided the city's youth with safe, structured programming designed to engage boys and girls in positive activities that improve their quality of life, present developmental opportunities, and offer the prospect of a brighter future. What started out as the closing of streets by the New York City Police Department to enable the city's unsupervised youth to have a place to play, became a city-wide "Cops & Kids" movement that eventually expanded into a national model that brought communities and the police together in ways that prevail to this day, for the betterment of both. Today the PAL boasts that it is "New York City's largest independent youth development not-for-profit organization and operates: Head-Start/day care; after-school and evening teen-summer-day camps; youth employment and truancy prevention; juvenile justice and re-entry into society; city-wide sports; play streets; part-time recreation centers; food services and adventure learning programs for pre-school kids. The programs are open to children and adolescents ages 3 to 19."

My journey with the PAL began when I was 15-years old. I was required to go to the 75th Police Precinct, on Miller and Liberty Avenues, to get a smallpox vaccination. Officer Maloney, the policeman that patrolled our neighborhood, and on many occasions told me to "Move along," saw me and took me to the station's gym. I was surprised to see many boys my age playing basketball, boxing and lifting weights. He asked if I would like to join the basketball players, I gladly did. It wasn't a game that I was good at, so he encouraged me to try out for the baseball team, and he even loaned me a ball and glove so I could practice. Practice I did, with my street-buddies who also were recipients of loaned gloves. Several of us ended up playing on the same PAL baseball team. I was lucky to play shortstop and was third at bat, which made me a very happy and important young boy. It was my first experience at willingly being committed to an event that required a team effort and added the synergy link to my every growing character-chain. We played many games on sand lots in different East New York neighborhoods, our major games were played with full uniforms at Highland Park, which is listed as a separate Zone on the "East New York Project" website. In the first summer season we placed second in our division and the following year we were honored with first place. An important character-link was added by winning and experiencing the thrill of being first; winning was fun and one way or another, there was always a reward in addition to the shiny trophies and medals we received.

Our reward for first place was a trip to the St. George Hotel in downtown Brooklyn. At the time it was the largest hotel in New York City, boasting over 2,600 rooms and rising 30 stories high with a rotating light beacon at the top that lit up the sky at night. It was a collection of buildings constructed between 1895 and 1929 that eventually occupied a full city block. The hotel was bounded by Clark Street, Pineapple Street, Hicks Street and Henry Street, and was so large and popular that the Clark Street-Brooklyn Heights subway station operated from below the hotel. So where is there a reward in going to a hotel? During excavation for its foundation, underground saltwater springs were discovered. They were tapped into and the largest indoor saltwater pool in the world was built, with a continuous flow of free natural sea water. Although the hotel no longer exists, the buildings that made up the complex have been recycled and now accommodates dormitories for local universities, a large gym, a small pool that is a remnant of the original, and business offices. It has the distinction of being a landmarked building in the first "Landmarked Neighborhood" in New York.

Our trip to the Clark Street-Brooklyn Heights' train station on the IRT Broadway-Seventh Avenue Line was my first journey out of my neighborhood into a city atmosphere. My only experience with far-away-places was Coney Island Beach, which required taking multiple trains, and to movie theatres that required taking trolley cars or busses. What a thrill exiting the train and entering the hotel's station; it looked like a palace. Starry eyed at the glittering tiled mosaic rounded walls, decorated with sailing ships and large named panels reading "Clark Street-Brooklyn Heights," we followed the mosaic tiles pointing and directing us to the St. George Hotel. The station was busy with an abundance of people traveling in every direction. I entered my first elevator-lift and was amazed at how quickly it got us to our destination above the train station. Following is a poster advertising the St. George Pool that is similar to the ones that were discreetly placed throughout the station and walkways:

There was so much splendor and activity around us, that I had trouble absorbing all of the surroundings. The ornate Art Deco lobby of the hotel looked more like the entrance to a royal palace. Red-coated bellhops greeted us and directed us through an arcade lined with pinball machines and aquatic pictures of swimming champions on its walls. I recognized two of my movie heroes, Johnny Weissmuller and Buster Crabbe, both of whom had played Tarzan in many adventure films that I had seen. There were shops throughout the arcade, similar to the ones found today in many of the larger upscale hotels. We entered the swimming pool area and were given a set of swim trunks, a towel and a locker key on an elastic band that could be secured on a wrist or ankle. All swimsuits were the same dark nondescript color; the girls at the pool were issued one piece black bathing suits that gracefully covered all of their important parts. From a distance we looked like a penguin colony, with penguins jumping in the air, moving about the pool area, and swimming and diving in every direction. We followed our leader to take mandatory showers in a huge room with private stalls. Although I had lived in four different dwellings up until that time, none of them had anything that resembled a full standup shower. The closest thing we had was a bathtub with a shower hose attached to the spout, so our showers consisted of a sitting down event after a bath. I must have spent half-an-hour in the shower stall, enjoying the stinging water hitting my body and soaping myself over and over again. Our coach came into the room and had to persuade several of us to leave our private temples. The swimming pool was something else. Looking at it from the overhead observation deck made it look like a mini-river to my boyish eyes. It measured 40 by 120 feet, with a 10-foot diving board abutted by three lower boards located at the 10-foot deep end of the pool. At the shallow end (3-feet) a waterfall splashed into the pool making sounds that complemented those of the bathers. Mosaic aquatic wall designs of fish and boats, separated by alternating mirrors and a series of supporting pillars faced with translucent green ceramic tiles, made the place seem infinite.

We were reminded by our guardian that we were on our "Good behavior" and that any rowdiness would result in our being kicked out of the premises.

Those words worked magic in our actions, as our anxiety at being in such an incredible place was starting to show in our restlessness. We spent several hours swimming, diving, racing and just enjoying being at a place we only imagined existed in Esther Williams' movie films. After we exhausted ourselves in the pool, our guardian escorted us to the air-conditioned gym where we completed exhausting ourselves until our actions became sluggish. The only exposure I had to air-conditioning was when I attended the movie houses in my neighborhood. I never dreamed that other places had the same comfort. I remember saying to myself "Soon they'll probably have air-conditioning in cars and houses," HO HO HO. . . . We ended our excursion with a mandatory return to the shower stalls, much to my delight, but we were only given five-minutes to complete our final wash; it would be many years before I set foot in a shower stall again.

For our good behavior that day, our coach took us to see an incredibly large television set in the lounge area of the hotel, it was probably about 60-inches, but to my inexperienced eyes it seemed like the size of a movie screen. Television sets were just beginning to appear in homes on very small black and white 12 inch screens. The sets were expensive and not easy to locate, so much so, that when I joined the United States Air Force in 1952, we still didn't have a TV set in our home.

The amazing day ended with our team physically and mentally exhausted. Physically from the swimming and gym workouts, and mentally from seeing sights that were to us out of a Buck Rogers' comic book or his science fiction movies. Many character-links were extended that day by the realization that there is a whole other world outside of my house and neighborhood. I learned that everyone has an opportunity to attain the better comforts of life, for a fee, and I learned not to be afraid to take chances. If I hadn't jumped off the 10-foot diving board (it seemed like 100 feet to me at the time), I would have never known that I was able to swim above and below the water for long distances. In my future, jumping in over my head and taking on new challenges became an important part of my persona.

As most teenagers, I was anxious to grow up and become an adult. So at age 16, several of my friends and I decided to join the National Guard to expedite our entrance into manhood. Of course we lied about our ages, as the required age for enlistment was 18. We joined the 69th Infantry Regiment of the 42nd Rainbow Division. The armory, which was built in 1906, is located at 68 Lexington Avenue between 25th and 26th Streets in the borough of Manhattan. It required taking two trains to get to the location, which took almost an hour. We spent many hours on Monday evenings and week-ends practicing our trade at the armory. Some of their Civil War battles engraved on the front of the huge building are: Bull Run, Va.; Antietam, Md.; Fredericksburg, Va.; Chancellorsville, Va.; Gettysburg, Pa.; Spotsylvania, Va., and the Appomattox Campaign, which led to the final capitulation by General Robert E. Lee of his Southern Forces to General Ulysses S. Grant at the Appomattox Court House in Virginia on April 9, 1865.

We were all assigned to the heavy mortar group. I would soon add responsibility and accountability to my character-chain from my experience in the "Fighting 69th" regiment, which got its name from no other then General Robert E. Lee during the Civil War. When asked what troops were facing his forces at the battle of Antietam, Maryland on September 17, 1862, he was told the 69th New York. His reply was, "Ah the fighting 69th." Americans sustained their highest death toll in a day in its military history; 23,000 men gave their lives on that hideous day. The name stuck and the memory of that battle and the others are well preserved in the Armory's Museum that depicts the history of the famous regiment in murals and pictures that adorn its walls. It was an Irish-heritage unit, with many of its traditions and symbols deriving from a time when the regiment was made up entirely of Irish-Americans, many of whom were born in Britain and Ireland. Reportedly, Company A/1st battalion was descended from the 8th Company of the 1st New York Regiment which was an American Revolutionary War Regiment. So there we were four Italian-Americans, Mike, Paul, John and Tom, enlisting in an Irish-dominated army unit that's nickname was "The fighting Irishmen." On the wall of honor at the museum are seven members of the regiment that were awarded the Medal of Honor, all survived the actions in which they were awarded the military's highest honor. They are listed as follows:

Peter Rafferty, Private, born in Ireland, received his award for action during the Civil War at Malvern Hill, Virginia, on July 1, 1862.

Citation: Having been wounded and directed to the rear lines, he declined to go, he continued in action, receiving several additional wounds while heroically battling the enemy.

Timothy Donoghue, Private, born in Ireland, received his award for action during the Civil War at Fredericksburg, Virginia, on January 17, 1864.

Citation: Voluntarily carried a wounded officer off the field from between the lines while wounded.

Joseph Keele, Sergeant Major, born in Ireland, received his award for action during the Civil War at North Anna River, Virginia on October 25, 1864.

Citation: Voluntarily and at the risk of his life carried orders to the brigade commander while under fire, which resulted in saving the important positions his regiment was defending.

Michael A. Donaldson, Sergeant, born in New York, received his award for action during WWI at Sommerance-Landres-et St. Georges Road, France on October 14, 1918.

Citation: The advance of his regiment having been checked by intense machine gun fire of the enemy, who were entrenched on the crest of a hill before Landres-et St. Georges, his company retired to a sunken road to reorganize their position, leaving several of their number wounded near the enemy lines. Of his own volition, in broad daylight and under direct observation of the enemy and with utter disregard for his own safety, he advanced to the crest of the hill, rescued one of his wounded comrades, and returned under heavy fire to his own lines, repeating his splendidly heroic act until he had brought in all six men.

William Joseph Donovan, Lieutenant Colonel, born in New York, received his award for action during WWI near Landres-et-St. Georges, France on October 14-15, 1918.

Citation: Lt. Col. Donovan personally led the assaulting wave in an attack upon a very strongly organized position, and when our troops were suffering heavy casualties he encouraged all near him by his example, moving among his men in exposed positions, reorganizing decimated platoons, and accompanying them forward in attacks. When he was wounded in the leg by machine-gun bullets, he refused to be evacuated and continued with his unit until it withdrew, to a less exposed position.

Richard W. O'Neill, Sergeant, born in New York, received his award for action during WWI on the Ourcq River in France, on July 30, 1918.

Citation: In advance of an assaulting line, he attacked a detachment of about 25 of the enemy. In the ensuing hand-to-hand encounter he sustained pistol wounds, but heroically continued in the advance, during which he received additional wounds; but, with great physical effort, remained in active command of his detachment. Being wounded he was forced by weakness and loss of blood to be evacuated, but insisted upon being taken first to the battalion commander in order to transmit to him the valuable information relative to the enemy positions and the disposition of the men.

Alejandro R. Renteria Ruiz, Private (not Irish), born in New Mexico, received his award for action during WWII in the battle of Ryukyu Island, Okinawa, on April 28, 1945.

Citation: When his unit was stopped by a skillfully camouflaged enemy pillbox, he displayed conspicuous gallantry and intrepidity above and beyond the call of duty. His squad, suddenly brought under a hail of machine gun fire and a vicious grenade attack, was pinned down. Jumping to his feet, Pfc. Ruiz seized an automatic rifle and lunged through the flying grenades, rifle, and automatic fire from the top of the emplacement. When an enemy soldier charged him, his rifle jammed. Undaunted, he whirled his assailant and clubbed him down. Then he ran back through bullets and grenades, seized more ammunition and another automatic rifle, and again made for the pillbox. Enemy fire now was concentrated on him, but he charged on, miraculously reaching the position and in plain view, climbed to the top and killed 12 of the enemy and completely destroyed their position. Pfc. Ruiz's heroic conduct, in the face of overwhelming odds, saved the lives of many comrades and eliminated an obstacle that long would have checked his unit's advance.

My buddies and I were overwhelmed with the history of the "Fighting 69th." We were now part of an organization that had extremely high standards we would have to meet. Becoming an adult was starting to get a little scary for us. But we were convinced that we were up to the job. Our ethnic backgrounds didn't interfere with our training, as a matter of fact, we learned many Irish customs, such as the use of the words to the 69th' battle cry, "Faugh a Ballagh;" which is Irish Gaelic for "Clear the Way." Our motto was "Gentle when stroked – Fierce when provoked," which was in reference to their mascot, the Irish Wolfhounds, who are proudly displayed on the unit's crest and dress cap badges which dates back to 1861. The Irish Wolfhounds are a living symbol of Irish culture and the Celtic past. These massive, muscular dogs weigh up to 150 pounds and are known as "The Great Hounds of Ireland." According to Irish lore and legend, their ancestors were guardians and companions of ancient kings and valued by Celtic chieftains as "Dogs of War," hence, their appearance on the 69th Regiment's insignia.

One of my most memorable recollections was marching in the famous St. Patrick's Day Parade up Fifth Avenue in full dress uniform proudly displaying my first stripe as a private. St. Patrick's Day is when everyone in New York City becomes Irish; the first parade was on March 17, 1762, 14 years before the Declaration of Independence was adopted. The annual parade is held on March 17, except if that date falls on a Sunday, then it's held the day before. It has been celebrated for almost 250 years in New York City, and is held to honor Ireland's patron saint, St. Patrick and the Archdiocese of New York. The parade is reviewed from the steps of St. Patrick's Cathedral by the sitting cardinal of the Catholic Church. It's regarded as the most popular true parade in New York City and the most famous one in the world. The parade starts at 44th Street at 11 AM and marches up Fifth Avenue past St. Patrick's Cathedral on 50th Street and past the Metropolitan Museum of Art and American Irish Historical Society on 83rd Street. It ends on 86th Street at approximately 4:30 PM. There are no floats in the parade, just marchers numbering upward to 300,000. The parade is headed by the "Fighting 69th Regiment" and followed by 32 Irish county societies, and various schools and college bands, emerald societies, Irish-language and nationalist organizations. It spreads out for over one-and-a-half-miles and is viewed by over three-million spectators. So there I was with my three Italian-American buddies marching at the head of the parade, just behind the Cavalry Brigade of the Fighting 69th. Fortunately the wind was blowing the horses' odors in the right direction, away from us, but occasionally there was a shift in the direction of the wind, which tested our discipline as soldiers and young boys, as the desire to break rank and run from the stench was very strong, but we held our places as good troop followers for over five hours. When we reached the end of the parade on 86th Street we fell out of our ranks and disbursed as far as possible from the horses. What a thrill it was being a part of such a massive endeavor. Soldiers from WWI and WWII filled our ranks and marched in the parade proudly wearing their uniforms and the many military decorations that they earned during their fighting days. Flags were flying, and bands were playing John Philip Sousa's marching music. Drums pounded the sounds directing our marching cadence and the horses in front of us marched perfectly, clippity clopping to the beat of the drums, occasionally raising their tails contributing their offensive droppings to the ambiance of the parade.

The "Fighting 69th" became a part of the 42nd Infantry Division in 1917, at the out-break of WWI, when its Chief of Staff Colonel Douglas MacArthur was asked to put together 26 National Guard units from different states and combine them into one fighting unit. He commented that the combined forces would resemble a rainbow, and hence the name became a part of the military's vocabulary when describing the 42nd Infantry (Rainbow) Division. Its patch has a green border, with a red, yellow and blue stripe. The famous division's patch follows:

The 69th Regiment's insignia has a gold border with a red clover, two golden Irish Wolfhounds touching a red and gold "69" with a red, gold, white and blue stripe running diagonally across the patch. The insignia follows:

The two catalysts for our enlisting in the National Guard during the Korean Conflict were the $15.00 a month check we would receive for serving in the military and the movie "The Fighting 69th." The 15 bucks was a lot of money to teenage boys in those days and represented a degree of financial freedom, and a brand new army uniform. We looked like grownups and wore our uniforms around the neighborhood with chests out, stomachs in and wide grins on our faces. We actually looked like the soldiers in the movie "The Fighting 69th" that starred James Cagney (every teenage boy's idol), playing Jimmy Plunkett, a smart-aleck kid from Brooklyn who was endowed with plenty of false bravado; his true colors show when he is in the battle of Argonne, in France, where bullets were flying around and grenades were exploding and decimating his regiment. He quickly shows his yellow-side, making mistakes that get many of his friends killed. For his cowardice he is sentenced to be shot by a military firing-squad. The most highly decorated priest in the history of the United States Army, Father Duffy, played by the actor Pat O'Brien, comes to his rescue and shows Jimmy the path to courageous behavior. In the end he redeems himself with gallant acts of bravery, but poetic justice was served at the end of the fictional movie, and for his cowardice that resulted in the deaths of many of his buddies, he himself is mortally wounded in action. What attracted us to the "Fighting Irishmen" were the actions of Father Duffy and the regimental commander, Lt. Colonel William "Wild Bill" Donovan, whose heroic acts won him the Medal of Honor in real life (see above Medal winners); the part was played by the dashing actor George Brent. Father Duffy has been memorialized with a monument in Duffy Square, which is located in the northern triangle of Times Square between 45th and 47th Streets in New York City. His statue stands in front of a Celtic cross that stands near 47th Street.

Being young teenagers we didn't realize the seriousness of our actions. We made adult decisions that required adult commitments. We had to attend roll-call every Monday evening at the Manhattan armory and spend two weeks in the summer at Camp Smith, which was the training grounds for New York State's National Guards; it's in Westchester County overlooking the Hudson River and across from the West Point Military Academy. Even though we were young boys, we were subject to disciplinary action for not adhering to military rules and regulations. After our indoctrination we were given books explaining the "Code of Military Conduct," which gave us our first inclination of how serious and dangerous our decision to join the National Guard was. The Korean War was in progress so we were eligible to be shipped overseas to join the United Nations' forces if the regiment was called-up to active duty. Our training at the armory during the year was in preparation for the two-weeks that we would spend at Camp Smith on military maneuvers. We were in the Heavy Mortar unit and were responsible for maintaining and using the 4.2 weapon. The M2 (4.2 inch mortar) is a rifled, muzzle-loading, high-angle-of-fire weapon used for long-range indirect fire support of infantry troops. It is 4-feet long and has a 4.2 inch barrel bore and weighs 333 pounds. Because of its size and weight, the weapon was used as regimental artillery and was usually vehicle mounted. A 4.2 mortar team had 8 men, with 4 squads, consisting of the track commander (mortar sergeant/gun commander), gunner, assistant gunner, loader and vehicle driver. My Italian-American buddies and I were separated and on different teams. Since we were the new guys on the block, we were all assigned the job of loaders on each of our teams. Well, what did the loader do? His job was to take the 25-pound projectile (shell) and drop it into the 4.2 inch opening of the barrel of the weapon and pray that it would exit the barrel as planned and would fly to its designated target. On more than one occasion the shell would be a dud and it was our job to retrieve it from the four-foot long barrel. How was this done? One of the gunners would separate the barrel from the base and lift it very slowly until the shell slid to the opening of the weapon. It was my job to catch the shell as it poked its head out of the barrel and very gently remove it. After that piece of work I would hand the smoking shell to the gunner who would quickly, but carefully, bring the shell to a waiting vehicle. The escape vehicle would take the shell and place it on the firing field where it became a target for our live ammunition. A picture of the M2 4.2 inch mortar follows:

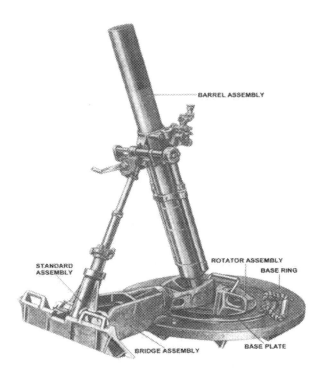

I was quickly adding links to my character-chain. I learned to never commit to something I didn't understand thoroughly. We all learned that accepting responsibility also meant accountability; there is no such thing as playing at being a grown-up; it was not a game but a serious and sometimes dangerous job.

Our unit's trip to Camp Smith was the first time that I left New York City. We were transported from the armory to the camp in military troop carriers consisting of hundreds of trucks traveling in a convoy formation; small jeeps led the way, then quarter-tracks, half-tracks and large equipment carriers bringing up the end of the line. It was exciting, I couldn't wait to begin my adult experience. We were billeted in one of the many barracks at the camp, sleeping on cots with upwards to a hundred men in each building. The latrines were a communal type set-up with no privacy. After settling in we marched to the Mess Hall (dining hall) and waited on line with hundreds of other soldiers until the food (mess) was finally dumped onto our metal trays; quality was not the order of the day, just quantities of nondescript food. The next day reveille was at 5:30 AM. The sound of the bugle through the loudspeakers blasted us out of beds and onto our feet. Half dazed, we dressed and were in formation in a matter of minutes. The plan for the day was to march and then run for an hour before we went to the Mess Hall for another nutritious meal. The day consisted of marching in the morning and the firing range in the afternoon, where we were taught how to handle and fire our new carbine rifles. Our experience with the weapon up until that point was dry-practice at the armory. Now we were going to fire live ammunition.

After familiarizing ourselves with the rifles we concentrated on learning how to handle our 4.2 inch mortars. We practiced from early morning until late afternoon in preparation of our War Games, which also required our tenting outdoors for the duration of the rivalry, which could be two to three days. We were the red team and were soundly defeated by the blue boys. The essence of the maneuvers was to expose us to real combat conditions with live ammunition flying and exploding around us. It was a miracle that no one was killed in the process. The objective of the teams was to see which one could reach a target area and blow up a small shelter. After the two-week camp experience we trucked back to our armory in Manhattan as reluctant adults. My Italian-American friends and I agreed that maybe we should have stayed teenagers a little longer, with a lot less responsibilities and certainly a lot less chance of being killed or wounded.

Although I didn't spend too much time attending classes in Junior High School, I somehow managed to finish and get a diploma. They were probably glad to get rid of me, so they expedited my exit. I didn't waste any time finding a job at age 15. My first attempt at full-time employment was with the now defunct Brooklyn Eagle newspaper as a delivery boy. Before I could start working for the newspaper I needed a bicycle. I didn't have enough money to buy one and I didn't want to ask my family for help as they were quite short of cash, so I went to the junk yard and put together a bike from scrap parts that I found lying around. At no charge to me, the yardman helped me put a pretty nice one together, except that the colors of the frame and each fender didn't match. He gave me a can of red paint and a brush so I could paint the whole bike the same color. He supervised my first painting experience and when I finished, the pride I felt matched the bright red color of my new bike. I was now ready to start my new job.

The pickup center for the paper was in my friend's extended basement which was a few blocks from where I lived. My day began at 5:30 AM and ended at 6 PM. I started with one route and after a couple of weeks they added a second route. If ever a job required commitment, delivering newspapers early in the morning in all kinds of weather was on top of the list. Their motto was, "Come rain, sleet, or snow; mud or flood, the Eagle always flies." I kept the job long enough to realize that there had to be an easier way to make money. My friend's father liked me and after I completed my routes, I would hang around and help him clean the basement and count the money that the paperboys brought in, and then calculate and disburse their pay-envelopes. I enjoyed working inside and learning a little about newspaper compilation and distribution, while earning some extra pocket money. At one point the Brooklyn Eagle was the most popular afternoon paper in the United States. It had such illustrious writers as Thomas Kinsella, St. Clair McKelway, Cleveland Rogers, Frank D. Schroth, Charles Montgomery Skinner and their most famous editor-writer, Walt Whitman. There were all sorts of memorabilia about the New York author of "Leaves of Grass" throughout the distribution center and the house. I picked up one of the many pamphlets about Whitman's life that were displayed in an honored place at the facility which read: "Walt Whitman is generally considered to be the most important American poet of the 19th century. He wrote in free verse (not in traditional poetic form), relying heavily on the rhythms of common American speech. He was born on May 31, 1819, in West Hills, Long Island, the second of nine children. His family soon moved to Brooklyn, where he attended school for a few years. Young Whitman took to reading at an early age. By 1830 his formal education was over, and for the next five years, beginning in 1836, he taught school on Long Island. During this time he also founded the weekly newspaper Long-Islander, (the paper still exists today). Many years after he was an editor and writer for the Brooklyn Eagle, he went to Virginia to find his brother George who was wounded in action during the Civil War. He was devastated when he witnessed the horrors of war and became a volunteer in military hospitals in Washington, DC, administering to the needs of the sick and wounded soldiers. He contracted 'hospital malaria' from his exposure to the sick servicemen and had to return to New York to recuperate. So upset was he by the war's devastation that he published 'Drum-Taps,' 'Cavalry Cross a Ford,' 'The Wound-Dresser,' 'Come Up from the Fields Father,' ' Vigil Strange I Kept on the Field One Night,' 'Sight in Camp in the Daybreak Gray and Dim,' and 'Year That Trembled and Reel'd Beneath Me'." Needless to say, I was quite impressed with his biography and promised myself that I would read his books and poems when I had time.

A friend of mine told me about a job he had on Wall Street delivering documents around Manhattan. He started work at 9 AM and was finished at 5 PM. He was earning almost double my salary and didn't have to get up early in the morning or travel during inclement weather. There was an opening at the company, so giving due notice to my boss at the Eagle, I began a new job in New York City working at Merrill Lynch, Pierce, Fenner & Beane, a large stockbrokerage firm on Wall Street, as a runner. My job was to deliver stock and bond certificates and other important documents around Manhattan. I loved the job as I made nice tips from the firms that I delivered papers to and met lots of interesting people; especially the many girls who thought that my red curly locks were a lucky charm and couldn't resist rubbing my head. What really fascinated me about the job was when it rained or snowed we would stay indoors and do menial tasks around the office, like filing documents or getting coffee and Danishes for the staff. The endless sounds from the ticker-tape-boards were spellbinding. The employees gladly answered the many questions I had about the financial market. The one thing I noticed was that not too many brokers or researchers had the same opinions about current or future performances of stocks being traded or about the economy. They would have morning meetings and decide what answers would be appropriate to questions that might be asked by customers that day about important issues in the financial markets. The answers were developed by consensus of opinion, of course the most dominating and experienced people always managed to have their opinions accepted and used for the day. A major link was added to my character-chain while working there that I would put to good use in my future dealings with stockbrokers and that is: a good deal of the information freely given by stockbrokers is purely guesswork, also I noticed that many brokers just churned their clients' accounts to keep their commissions rolling in. Some of the sayings that I heard while working in the office were: "Don't fall in love with a stock, as it can't love you back." "There are three types of investors, the Bulls, the Bears and the Pigs." "If we knew what we were talking about we would all be millionaires and probably working for ourselves," and the most famous of all, "Buy low and sell high," this saying was attributed to Bernard Baruch, master financier of the 20th century, when someone asked him how to make money in the stock market. Another of his quotes, which I used throughout my life is "Every man has a right to his opinion, right or wrong, but no man has a right to be wrong in his facts." These sayings just about describe the lack of depth and honesty of some brokers' knowledge when it comes to picking stocks objectively and considering the customer's interests first. Reading the Kiplinger Financial Newsletter was a ritual at the firm. I remember a challenge that Kiplinger gave to its followers, defying them to beat his past year's stocks performances, which was exceptionally good, by choosing stock for the next quarter and comparing the customers' results to his firm's. Well, some of the boys got together and randomly chose 12 securities for the forthcoming quarter. When the results were in we didn't beat Kiplinger's exceptional results but we did match their performance percentage gains. Our results were based solely on random choices of stocks in the daily New York Times financial pages. A lesson well learned and put to good use in the future for all of us.

The building I worked in housed a history museum of the innovative company. Charles E. Merrill and his partner Edmund C. Lynch opened their doors in 1914 as Merrill, Lynch & Co. They directed their efforts and attention in later years to "Putting the customer's interest first." With proper training of their employees they stressed, "Our mission is to bring Wall Street to Main Street America and we can only do this by putting our customers' interests above our own." They proudly boasted of having the first female, Annie Grimes, as their operations manager and saleswoman. A highlight, and one of the proudest moments in their illustrious career, was predicting the stock market crash of 1929, and warning their clients and partners to get out of the stock market and into government bonds. Merrill even warned President Calvin Coolidge about the possible market collapse, but his warning fell on deaf ears. The firm not only weathered the storm but experienced a period of rapid expansion while other businesses vanished. In 1938 Lynch died at age 52, and in deference to his partner, Merrill had the comma taken off of Merrill, Lynch & Co. In the 1940's, various mergers with other brokerage houses made Merrill Lynch, Pierce, Fenner & Beane the largest securities house in the world, with a motto of, "The interest of the customers MUST come first." In the same decade they were responsible for the first woman to work on the floor of the New York Stock Exchange. One memorable occasion happened to me when I was visiting the museum on a rainy day; a gentleman tapped me on the shoulder and asked me what I was doing? I said: "Reading the information about the company." He said: "Why are you in this building?" I answered: "I work here as a runner." He said: "Why aren't you in school?" I said: "I quit so I could work." He said: "Foolish boy," and then he left shaking his head. I found out later that the slightly built, gray haired gentleman was no other than Charles E. Merrill himself. I couldn't understand why a total stranger would use the exact words that my father and relatives had been saying since my rebellious actions of quitting school and going out into the world to expedite my entrance into adulthood. Those two words "Foolish boy" would haunt me for many years to come.

On the leisure side of my life at that time were playing baseball, girls and horseback riding. My National Guard buddies and I walked about a mile to the stables on New Lots Avenue and paid a dollar each to ride horses for an hour. In time we became friendly with the owner, he would give us free riding time if we tended the horses, which included brushing their muscular frames, cleaning debris from their hooves and feeding them. We would spend every free moment of our time at the stables, especially enjoying the night-riding where we would end up on the beach with campfires and sing-along songs, just like real cowboys, who we were convinced we were. We always enjoyed having girls on the outings as they had better singing voices than the boys and would always have great picnic baskets of food prepared for our consumption. They also smelled a lot better than the horses or the guys. The owner had a horseback riding concession at Coney Island and asked me if I would like to work there the following summer. I quickly said yes, the only problem was that I needed a car to get there as the train ride required two transfers and over an hour to arrive early in the morning. So my objective for the year was to save enough money to buy a car, even though I was too young to get a driver's license, but in those days not having a license wasn't important for a teenager as we made up our own rules as we went along.

I saved fifty-dollars at Merrill and bought a 1936 convertible Ford with a rumble seat in the back. With the use of my "new" car, and no driver's license, I was able to drive to Coney Island and spend the summer at my dream job. A picture of a classic 1936 convertible Ford with a rumble seat follows; of course the one I bought was not in the same condition as the beauty in this picture:

I tended my resignation at Merrill and couldn't wait to begin my Coney Island journey. My "new" car needed lots of body work. The front fenders were dented and rusted, so my immediate job was to restore them to "like new" condition. I banged out the dents and sanded the rust out of the metal until the fenders were down to their original steel. I went to the local hardware store to get some black paint so I could turn the jalopy into a respectable looking hotrod. The store owner showed me a new invention, spray-can-paint. He said it didn't leave any brush stroke marks and if I sanded between coats the finish would be the same as on a "new" car. My eye caught a strange color that I had never seen called chartreuse, which the hardware man told me was a mixture of yellow and green. Wow!! Would my hotrod look great with the front fenders in that color!! I bought the necessary spray-cans and followed the instructions meticulously. I gave the fenders three shiny coats each and then polished them to perfection. Then I cleaned and painted the tires black with a three inch white stripe on them, (I probably started a new trend), then I compounded and polished the black body with Simonize until I could clearly see my reflection. Next I scrubbed the white convertible top until it was almost pure white and touched up any unwanted blemishes with white paint. After weeks of preparation, and lots of hard trial-and-error work, my jalopy was transformed into the best looking hotrod in Brooklyn. I immediately was the most popular teenager in the neighborhood, adding some additional links to my character-chain such as, it's easy to make friends if you have something they want, and most importantly, girls "Love" cars. . . .

What more did a teenager need? I had a car that gave me the freedom to travel wherever I pleased without relying on anyone else. I had a pair of Levi dungarees and a new macho black leather jacket. A picture of that happy teenager with lots of red wavy hair follows:

My job at the riding concession consisted of holding the horse's or pony's reins while walking riders around the small track. I did this for ten hours a day, seven days a week from June till September. When it wasn't busy the other riding assistants and I would rotate shifts which gave me lots of time to explore Coney Island. One of the fringe benefits of working on the boardwalk was that when other concessionaires got to know you, their wares and goodies were free in exchange for helping them clean up or doing odd chores. I had many free hotdogs, corns-on-the-cobs, BBQ steak sandwiches, French-fries and cokes at Nathan's Famous hot dog stand. I was also able to ride the Cyclone, Parachute Jump, Wonder Wheel and many other rides, free of charge. One of the most enjoyable events was lying around on the beach while meeting pretty young girls who thought I was the king of the midway because I worked in carnival-land. One of the less pleasurable events was that when I returned home in the evenings, I had to strip down and leave my clothing in the hallway, and jump into the tub-shower to try to remove the aroma that I carried home from working at the stables. After a couple of weeks, my father and I agreed that it would be okay for me to occasionally sleep in one of the backrooms of the stable. This made life a lot easier on me and my sister Anne who was responsible for washing my clothing in addition to her raising my nephew Dennis, holding a part time job, and trying to perform her other household chores. I bought an extra pair of dungarees and occasionally used the Laundromat at Coney Island to get the stiffness out of my Levi's; this solved both of our problems. She didn't have to touch my ripe clothing and I didn't have to go through the ritual of disrobing before entering our home every night, as a matter of fact, if my memory serves me, there were times that I slept in my cowboy outfit for more than one day while staying in the back room of the stable. It was odd that no one that worked in the carnival complained that I didn't meet the cleanliness standards of my family. I guess we all shared a common fragrance.

Sleeping in Coney Island gave me an opportunity to explore the never-ending fascinating places along the Boardwalk, Surf Avenue, Steeplechase Amusement Park and the Bowery. Coney Island is a peninsula in the southernmost part of the Borough of Brooklyn and is landlord to one of the world's most beautiful beaches. It extends from the exclusive private neighborhood of Seagate to its west; Brighton Beach and Manhattan

Beach to its east; and Gravesend to the north. It became a resort after the Civil War as excursion railroads and the Coney Island and Brooklyn railroad streetcar lines reached the area in the 1860's. With easy access to the beach area came major hotels, horse racing, amusement parks, and less reputable entertainment, such as, the Three-card Monte street hustle, a variety of gambling establishments, street hucksters and prostitution. At the beginning of the 20th century, Coney Island turned from what was considered an upscale resort to an accessible location for day-trippers from the five boroughs seeking to escape from the summer's heat by using the magnificent beach that extended from West 37th Street at Seagate, through Coney Island, Brighton Beach, and on to the beginning of the communities of Manhattan Beach, a distance of approximately 2½ miles. The Riegelmann Boardwalk ran the whole length of the beach and had a number of amusement and refreshment stands on and around the boardwalk. A modified street map follows that locates many of the parks and famous streets of Coney Island at that time:

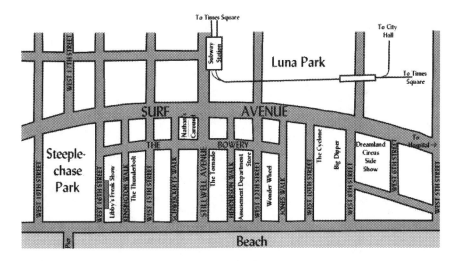

From 1885 to 1896, the Coney Island Elephant was the first sight to greet immigrants arriving to New York. It was a giant elephant known as the "Elephantine Colossus," and stood 122 feet high with seven floors and 31 rooms. A renowned hotel and brothel, in its short history it accommodated some of New York's elite with a variety of sinful activities. It met a similar fate as many of the popular places in Coney Island when it burned down in 1896, never to be rebuilt again. Between 1880 and the end of WWII, Coney Island was the largest amusement area in the world, attracting millions of visitors a year. Within that time period, it contained three competing major amusement parks: Luna Park, Dreamland Park, and Steeplechase Park. In addition it had many independent smaller amusement parks and concessions lined up on Surf Avenue, the Bowery and the surrounding streets.

The first park to open in Coney Island was Steeplechase Amusement Park in 1897, which still existed when I worked there, (it was closed in 1964). It was one of the most influential amusement parks in the industry's history, and was used as a model for other fun-parks throughout the world. Diminutive pictures of Coney Island and Steeplechase Park follows; in the first picture the Merry-go-round is in the forefront, the Cyclone to the left, Parachute Jump and Wonder Wheel are in the background:

One of the master builders of Coney Island and specifically Steeplechase was George Cornelius Tilyou. In 1862, his father Peter Tilyou leased a huge 300 foot wide ocean front lot for $35.00 a year and built the Surf House, a place that served food and rented bathing attire to visitors. From the beginning his son George showed his genius by selling "Authentic Salt Water" in bottles and "Authentic Beach Sand" in cigar boxes to gullible tourists for twenty-five cents each. George took the profits from his operation and reinvested it in real estate in the area and built Coney Island's first theater, Tilyou's Surf Theater, along an alley that bisected the walk streets between Surf Avenue and the Atlantic Ocean. To make sure customers had easy access to the theater through the cluster of beer saloons, clam bars, bathhouses and muddy streets, he paved an alley with wooden planks. When the planked road was completed the area resembled the notorious Manhattan Bowery, hence, that is where the name of the street that I walked got its name, "The Bowery." A 1908 picture of the reopening of Steeplechase from the planked Bowery follows:

The first Steeplechase was destroyed by fire in 1907 and promptly rebuilt by George for the 1908 summer season. This time the structures had to be built within the new safety ordinances which banned wood, and required that steel, glass, concrete and other noncombustible materials be used in the reconstruction; which is probably why most of the park was intact when I walked and played within its confines forty-plus years later. The attractions that I remember so well were: the "Ferris Wheel," the One Ring "Circus," and my favorite; the two "Horse Race Tracks," which consisted of a high track and a lower track. Each track had four horses seating two riders each, racing along guided rails parallel to each other. The high track was a slightly longer course, approximately 1700-feet with a higher starting point, and traveled one lap around the exterior of the "Pavilion of Fun" building. The 1600-foot-long inner track with a lower starting point ran under the colonnade roof on the side of that building. The riders' horses were drawn up on a cable to an elevation of 22-feet at the start of the race, and quickly dropped downward along a 15% grade track to gain speed. The riders then rode across a miniature lake, while their momentum carried them upwards again to the height of 16-feet above the beach, the riders then descended through a tunnel and raced upward over a series of jolts until they reached the finish line. Heavier riders usually had the advantage of winning, as their weight moved the horses down the ending slopes at a faster pace than lighter riders. At the end of the ride racers were led to the "Pavilion of Fun's Insanitarium" and "Blowhole Theater." Riders entered the stage on their hands and knees through a low doghouse where a cowboy, a tall farmer and a dwarf clown awaited them and guided them through an alley called "Comedy Lane." While the hosts distracted the victims, a system of compressed-air jets would blow men's hats and toupees off their heads and send women's skirts flying upward to the embarrassment of many of the girls, and to the amusement of the audience. The clown's job was to prod the man's buttocks with an electric stinger; when his girlfriend would reach out to help the stunned guy, the clown would shoot a blast of air under her dress and watch it soar as the audience roared with laughter. The mortified couple would hurry by six-foot-high playing cards, a tree with six-foot-long hotdog branches and a dwarf clown who swatted them with slapsticks. Finally the couple would reach a moveable floor known as "Battleship Roll." Piles of barrels on either side of the walkway would begin to shake and appear to be falling down on them as they scrambled for safety, finally escaping into the audience. The exhausted racers then had an option to leave or, at no charge, to sit in the audience and enjoy the next groups' embarrassing encounters with the clowns. Some girls would repeat their performance several times during the day wearing colorful undergarments that they would change each time as if to tell the audience, who's laughing now!!!

I wrote extensively about the Race Track Ride because it was the most popular attraction in Steeplechase and the ride that I most often either participated in or watched as a spectator in the comfortable seats of the theater. The list of rides and their purpose could fill two books; therefore, I'll only list some that I enjoyed while spending my memorable summer working in "Fantasyland." In Steeplechase there was the "Mixer," it was a big revolving platform, 30-feet in diameter with room for up to 24-people. As it spun faster and faster it catapulted riders into its surrounding scoop like bowl. A one-of-a-kind, "Chicken Carousel," had 38 chickens, and 14 ostriches instead of horses. The ride was as popular as its sister, the Horse Carousel, and thrilled children of all ages that rode on their enormous backs. Another carousel, the "El Dorado," which was salvaged from the 1911 Dreamland Amusement Park's fire, was a special attraction and ride as it contained a menagerie of animals on three platforms arranged in ascending tiers, each revolving at different speeds. Its crown-like canopy rose to a height of 42-feet and was illuminated with 6,000 lamps that enhanced the appearance of its horses, pigs, cows and other barnyard animals. Watching riders enjoying themselves on the backs of the strange looking animals was one of the funniest scenes in Coney Island. I had two other favorite places at the park where I spent many a relaxing hour; they were the fenced "Private Beach" in front of Steeplechase which was for the use of its paying customers, or special freeloaders like me, and the world's largest outdoor salt water pool, which held 670,000 gallons of water. Free ocean water fed the 270-foot long and 90-foot wide outdoor mini-man-made-lake, which housed two large bathing platforms on either side of its length. The pool could accommodate over a thousand bathers who took advantage of swimming, diving, jumping or just relaxing in or hiding from the sun. I was proud to brag that I swam in the world's largest indoor salt water pool at the St. George Hotel, and the world's largest outdoor salt water pool at Steeplechase Park. The park also had many rides and swimming places for small children, in addition to the multitude of imaginative assorted fun and thrill rides. Unfortunately after my short excursion to the park, it was closed in 1964. Till this day, I don't think there is an amusement park that can compare to the sophistication and variety of rides that Steeplechase had in its heyday.

The second major amusement park to be built was Luna Park; it lasted from 1903 to 1944 when it disappeared in a roaring fire that destroyed the park beyond repair. While it existed it claimed that in one year they had almost five-million visitors using their astonishing themed attractions. Amusement park historians claim that it was the precursor of Disneyland's themed parks. Elmer "Skip" Dundy and Frederick Thompson created a cyclorama (pictorial) ride called "A Trip to the Moon," and exhibited it at the Pan-American Exposition which was held in Buffalo, New York in 1901. When George Tilyou saw the amazing attraction he asked the two men to have it moved to Steeplechase after the exposition ended. They agreed and recreated their masterpiece in that park in 1902. After a successful year, they decided to purchase land on Surf Avenue and build their own amusement park, hence, Luna Park was born. They accumulated over 38-acres adding a variety of themed attractions to their empire, which made them a serious competitor for Steeplechase. They made enough money in their first year of operation to pay all of their debt and returned a handsome profit to their investors. My Aunt Amelia, on my mother's side, took me and her daughter, my cousin Anna, to the park when I was about nine-years old. A picture of the entrance in 1903 on Surf Avenue follows:

With a little research and lots of mind searching, I remembered the ride "A Trip to the Moon" that we went on with our eyes wide open in disbelief of the spectacular attraction, and our minds dazed at the possibility of taking a simulated trip to the moon. We entered the extravagant lobby where we waited with bated breath for our turn to enter the craft's dock which had a large holding-room. Absorbing the night view of the brightly lit green and white cigar-shaped "Luna" spaceship was one of my scariest and exciting childhood moments. To a child's eyes it seemed to be a mile long, with massive red canvas wings stretched out above its large cabin. Thirty passengers were ushered aboard the craft and directed to oversized seats. A large gong sounded announcing that "Luna's" huge wings were starting to slowly rise and fall, while the ship's floor began to vibrate. There was a rush of wind as the ship's heavy cables moved the craft up and down giving us the feeling that it was taking-off. As it flew higher into space we could see the Earth as a globe that rapidly decreased in size. Although the scenery was painted on movable canvas, it was real to a boy of nine; I imagined that we were actually in outer-space. The spaceship reached the moon in record time; it flew past canyons and craters stained yellow, green and red. The wings slowed their flapping and we landed in the crater of a volcano on the moon. We were greeted by green midget moon-men, whose backs had rows of long spikes sticking out. They sang "My Sweetheart the Man in the Moon." We were escorted through caverns, and across chasms spanned by spidery bridges to the underground "City of the Moon." We then entered the "Moon Castle" which led to the throne room where we sat in the Earth Visitors' Section. Bronze griffins flanked the sides of a giant "Man in the Moon'" who was seated on his gigantic throne. He greeted us in a deep powerful voice while moon maidens in green offered us "Green Cheese," (in those days it was rumored that the moon was made of green cheese), which tasted like mint cotton candy. At the end of the outer-space experience we exited past a colorful electrified fountain that danced to musical tunes and seemed to whisper, "Come back for another scare, if you dare." We walked out through the mouth of an enormous "Moon-Calf" into the park's welcoming daylight that quickly brought me back to reality.

We were anxious to get to the beach and go swimming, which worked out well for my Aunt Amelia, as I'm sure she couldn't afford to spend any more money on the many attractions at the park. We did get to see some live elephants and camels that were escorted throughout the grounds and were able to sit at a picnic table and eat the delicious eggplant and meatball sandwiches on Italian bread that she made, complemented by lemonade she lovingly prepared for us. My mother gave me a dollar, so I treated all of us to custard ice cream cones; I actually had change left over after paying the tab. An interesting aside is when I was in my forties there was a commercial venture that was advertising "A First" civilian trip to outer-space for a fee of twenty-five thousand dollars. I immediately signed up and sent a five-thousand dollar deposit to hopefully secure a seat on the rocket ship. The journey included a month's pre-flight training in Texas and then on to the space flight experience. Well, needless to say, Barbara was livid. She said: "How could you risk your life, we have two children, have you lost your mind?" All of the above were correct, but I couldn't get my Luna Park experience and the exhilaration from that incredible farsighted venture out of my mind. Fortunately for all of us, the first rocket test failed dismally, and in short order the adventure was cancelled and my deposit returned.

The excitement and splendor of Luna Park would not be soon forgotten. In May of 2010 a new Luna Park resurrected on the former Astroland site in Coney Island, which was closed in 2008. The new park is located on 8th Street on the oceanside of Surf Avenue directly across the street from the original park. Mayor Bloomberg of the city of New York proudly headed the opening ceremony dedicating the new Playland to the people of the five boroughs of New York City and to all the millions of visitors from around the world who will come and enjoy its amazing fun-rides. The mayor said "I can't wait to stand on line at Nathans Famous hotdog stand which is just a few blocks away, for a serving of my soul food, foot-long hotdogs and fried potatoes."

The rides for the park were made by the world's leading amusement park manufacturer, Zamperla of Venice, Italy. Some of the 19-rides are: the "Air Race" where riders pilot their own planes around a "control tower pole" while they spin, flipping head over heals in barrel rolls. The "Surf's Up" ride allows riders to balance on a surfboard and ride a 90-foot wave. The "Tickler" which is modeled after the original Luna Park's Tickler, rotates cars in circles as they speed over the coaster track's twists and turns. The "Electro Spin" is a combination spinning ride and coaster where riders sit facing outward on a spinning platform that travels back and forth along a U-shaped track. The "Eclipse" swings riders back and forth on a spinning platform into an almost frenzy and the "Lunar Express" which is devoted to entertaining small children and family members. The following year new rides will be added in the "Scream Zone" which will include two giant steel roller coasters, one with upside down loops. They plan on having go-karts and a human slingshot that will launch riders 200 feet in the air. The park's grand entranceway festooned with crescent moons is similar to the one that I saw as a young boy and that millions of visitors from around the world passed through in the first half of the 20th century. A promotion poster authored by Newkai was taken from Wikipedia Commons and is presented below:

The third major amusement park was Dreamland, which opened in 1904 and closed in 1911 due to a devastating fire that wiped out the entire park and put all the attractions on Surf Avenue at risk. I never saw Dreamland as it was before my time on earth, but I'm writing about it to give the flavor and imagination of Coney Island's atmosphere when all three parks were operating at the same time, creating the largest and most imaginative amusement site in the world. The information that I gathered comes mainly from Wikipedia: "It was built as a high-class entertainment park with elegant architecture, pristine white towers and some educational exhibits, along with thrill rides and upscale eating establishments. It was reputed to have one million electric light bulbs illuminating and outlining its buildings—quite an innovation at that time, thanks to Thomas Edison's supervision of the installation of the dazzling lights.

Among Dreamland's attractions were a railway that ran through a Swiss alpine landscape; imitation Venetian canals with gondolas; a 'Lilliputian Village' with three hundred dwarf inhabitants, and a demonstration of firefighting in which two hundred people pretended to put out a blazing six-story building, (their practice didn't help prevent the park's demise). There was also a display of baby incubators, where premature babies were cared for and exhibited. The story of the first premature triplet infants is very interesting. They were members of the Dicker family, who were owners of some of the concessions in the park. Doctors advised them of the new invention, which they could not use because incubators were not approved for use in hospitals. So the triplets were placed in the incubators as a side show, which was allowed. Miraculously, two of them survived and lived to have full lives." A picture of the entrance to Dreamland Amusement Park on Surf Avenue in 1905 follows:

2066   ENTRANCE TO DREAMLAND, CONEY ISLAND. N. Y.   ILL. POST CARD CO., N. Y.

The fourth amusement park was where the many independent concessioners had rides and attractions throughout Coney Island. Some popular ones were shooting galleries, miniature horse races, the strongman bell challenge, guess your age games, guess your weight games, throw the ring games and win a doll, toss a penny into a hole and win a prize, a pony and horse ride (my job), girlie shows, bars and grills up and down almost every street along Surf Avenue, bumper cars, and of course, the many eating places from upscale dining in Luna and Steeplechase parks to Nathan's Famous hotdog stand, Nedick's juice and hotdog stand, soft custard ice cream stands, and on and on. . . . A never ending place to spend an hour, a day, a week or a month eating, drinking, and enjoying the fun and thrill rides. One of my favorite part-time jobs when not attending the ponies was collecting tickets at the girlie shows, which were only a couple of blocks from where I worked. I made a deal with the ticket-takers to watch their booths while they took breaks; my reward was free entry to the girlie shows, even though I was underage. I certainly met lots of interesting people at those joints.

One of my biggest problems that summer was keeping myself relatively clean, especially after a couple of days tending the ponies at the stable. My problem was solved in a place called Ravenhall Baths which was next door to Steeplechase and bordered its property on West 19th Street. It had a swimming pool almost as large as the one at Steeplechase, showers, steam rooms, a gym, lockers and lunch counters. A picture of Steeplechase's Pool with the Wonder Wheel in the background follows:

On rainy days when we couldn't show our ponies and the swimming pool was closed, I would use my special "freeloading" privileges and meet my buddies who worked at the baths. I would shower and use the facilities as if I was a member, to get myself in hygienic and presentable condition. There were Bryle Cream hair tonic dispensers in the wash rooms for their customers, which I made good use of, as it was strong enough to keep my red-curly-unruly-hair under control. After making myself presentable for public display, we would usually mosey along to Steeplechase where we would use our "freeloading" privileges to enter and use their indoor "Pavilion of Fun" facilities to help pass the time of day, while relaxing and having a great time. After its first fire in 1907, Tilyou rebuilt the "Pavilion of Fun" as a glass and steel indoor amusement park. It covered five-acres with such exotic rides as "The Pipe," which was a covered slide where riders would climb to the top of the stairs and speed down inside the pipe crashing to the cushioned pavilion floor; "The Human Pool Table," which was a large flat surface made up of 24 large rotating discs that revolved in opposite directions challenging players to move from one surface to another without falling and becoming entangled with each other; "The Human Roulette Wheel" spun until passengers sitting on it were flung to the perimeter, and "The Human Zoo" where visitors descended a spiral staircase until they found themselves in a cage, where they were offered peanuts and monkey talk. These attractions and others were more than enough to keep a young teenager busy until dinner time or until the sun came out and the pony rides resumed.

I am proud to boast that I frequently enjoyed three rides at Coney Island that are now on the National Register of Historic Places. According to Wikipedia they are, "The 'Wonder Wheel' which was built in 1918. This steel Ferris wheel has both stationary cars and rocking cars that slide along a track. It holds 144 riders, stands 150 feet tall, and weighs over 2,000-tons. At night the Wonder Wheel's steel frame is outlined and illuminated by neon tubes. Today it's part of Deno's Wonder Wheel Amusement Park. The 'Cyclone' roller coaster, built in 1927, is one of the nation's oldest wooden coasters still in operation. A favorite of many coaster aficionados, it boasts as being 85-feet high and has a 60-degree drop. It is owned by the City of New York and is operated by Astroland, under a franchise agreement. It's located across the street from Astroland Amusement Park in Coney Island. The 'Parachute Jump,' originally the Life Savers Parachute Jump at the 1939 New York World's Fair, was the first ride of its kind. Patrons were hoisted 190-feet in the air before being allowed to drop, using guy-wired parachutes. Although the ride has been closed since 1968, it remains a Coney Island landmark and is sometimes referred to as 'Brooklyn's Eiffel tower.' Between 2002 and 2004, the jump was completely dismantled, cleaned, painted and restored, but remains inactive. After an official lighting ceremony in July 2006, the Parachute Jump was slated to be lit year round using different color motifs to represent the seasons. However, the idea was scrapped when New York City started conserving electricity in the summer months."

Well, as all good things must come to an end, the Disneyesque journey was over and I headed back to reality in my old neighborhood in East New York. Some of the concessionaires were moving south for the winter and asked if I would like to join them, a difficult decision for a young boy to make. The thought of roaming freely with circus-type people, and all the pretty girls that never got tired of rubbing my red-wavy-hair, was tempting. After much thought (about two minutes) I wisely declined. My friends threw me a going-away beach party on my last night in playland. Lulu from the girly show, Johnny from Steeplechase, Frankie from the bath house, my boss from the pony ride and many other acquaintances came to say goodbye to the young redhead. We roasted hotdogs, potatoes and marshmallows, while friends played their guitars, harmonicas and tambourines, and sang "You are my Sunshine," "Life's a Bowl of Cherries," and other popular songs of that time. Before the festivities ended, it seemed like everyone in Coney Island came to say goodbye. I've always been amazed at Coney Island at night. It seems as if all the attractions put on their "Sunday Best," all dolled up and showing off their brilliance in the form of colorful lights. The Wonder Wheel, which in the daytime just looked like a large circle with no personality, all of a sudden was bright and illuminated, a sparkling presence, outshining all the other attractions as it turned and its multicolored lights changed positions with each other, giving it the appearance of being the main source of energy in the park, and that every other display revolves and is energized by it. Right behind it was the Parachute Jump, which seems to be an inanimate object in the daytime; it lights up at night, and resembles a rocket ship ready for takeoff into outer space. Its brilliant sparkling lights made it the highest focal point in the park. It was the last time that I would experience Coney Island's sparkling night views, the unique mixed scents from its tenants, the invigorating saltwater air, the beige sand nestling between my toes, the smiling faces of my jolly friends, and the camaraderie of the most amazing collection of rainbowed personalities to be found on this planet. I forced myself to hold back the tears that were forming in my mind and would soon escape through my eyes; my young macho persona allowed me to leave before the cascade began. The evening and my summer adventure in Coney Island ended with hugs and kisses, and some tears from the gals, and promises from everyone to keep in touch. . . . If not in this life then we surely would in the next.

I carried home with me many new links to my character-chain. Getting along with people of different ethnic and religious groups was the most profound. Before my venture, most of my friends were Italian Americans. Now I had many Irish-Catholics, German-Protestants, Polish-Catholics-Protestants, Afro-Americans, Native Americans and Jews from Germany, Russia, Poland, Spain and even Italy. What a blessing that summer was for a teenage boy that fortunately became colorblind due to meeting so many people from different ethnic backgrounds and learning to get along with them on a daily basis. Our parents seemed to be different from us and each other, they all were burdened with historical baggage and trapped into traditional beliefs and dislikes. We on the other hand were the enlightened generation, born in America, we were all Americans; we dressed alike, spoke the same language with the same Brooklyn inflection without a hint of a foreign accent, had similar interests and didn't care about each other's religion or heritage. As a matter of fact, most of us wanted to see the world a better place for everyone, regardless of race, religion or political beliefs; we just wanted to have fun.

I was able to save almost all of my earnings from my meager salary, which when accumulated was a considerable amount of money at that time; I also saved the generous tips I received from parents for escorting their children safely on the pony rides. All the savings gave me a feeling of being independently rich. Dealing with the general public, learning to be patient, and controlling my temper, which at times was violent, was another well learned lesson. Learning to deal socially and to become friends with vendors who were competitors was a major step forward for me and would be put to good use in my future business dealings.

A friend of mine was working in Brooklyn at Sterling Casket Hardware and told me there was an opening with a good starting salary. The job was spraying paint on casket handles and then making decorative freehand designs. I got the job and was able to drive to work every day in under a half-an-hour. Gas at that time was 17-cents a gallon, so the cost of traveling to and from work was inexpensive. Driving to work certainly added to my independent spirit and my will to be a responsible adult. A vivid memory of the job was that after lunch each day, the crew of sprayers would take turns napping in the soft silk coffins that were on display in the showroom, certainly a prelude to a future happening in our lives. I stayed at the job for a few months and then took a job at Appeal Printing in Manhattan as a shipping clerk and truck dispatcher. The job was at a higher salary and didn't require using my jalopy that was starting to weaken after 15-years on the road. From that point on I only used it for dating girls, going to the horseback riding academy on Linden Boulevard, and getting my friends to our baseball games with the PAL. On weekends, to earn extra money, I helped my brother-in-law Lou Ambrico, who owned and operated a funeral hearse, transport dead bodies to the undertaker's hall for embalming and beautification. It was probably the worst job I ever had, but I continued working with him as it put lots of extra bucks in my pocket. The most depressing part of the job was dealing with a relative's grief when we had to remove their loved one's body. That job probably added one of the most important character-links to my chain. Many of the cadavers that we picked up were young, as well as elderly, and it made me realize how precious life is and to appreciate and not take loved ones for granted, for tomorrow may never come for them or me.

While working in the printing company, I had an experience that would come back to taunt me forty years later. Near the end of the day, my supervisor Sal sent me to the warehouse, which was below our printing plant and offices, to get some irregular sized cardboard shipping boxes. It took me quite a while to locate the small boxes and when I went to leave the warehouse, the door was locked. So, there I was locked inside without a cell phone (they weren't invented yet) and no other phone on the premises. To make things worse, the lights went off and the switch to turn them back on was in the outside hall. Today we have telephones in every conceivable location in the work place, but in those days phones were a luxury and only placed where needed. After pounding the door for what seemed to be an eternity, I realized that it was well past quitting time and everyone had left for the day. There was a fire-ax on the wall, which I immediately took and was ready to use on the wooden door, when I realized that if the police arrived and caught me in action, I would probably spend the night in jail, until they could verify the next morning that I was a victim of an unusual situation (that now seems very funny). I made myself comfortable and spent the night sleeping on some cardboard cartons that I just couldn't get to resemble the feeling of the nice mattress that was in my bedroom at home. I also used the cartons as a cover to keep me warm. In the middle of the night I heard the activity of critters, probably rats and mice, crawling and squealing around the warehouse. I took the largest box and enclosed myself inside it. Talk about being scared; when daylight came their sounds vanished and I was finally able to get some shuteye. I turned over in my mind how I would explain to my father and sister Anne the reason for my not coming home that evening; I just couldn't come up with a rational explanation. . . .

In the morning the warehouse door opened and my supervisor Sal came in and wanted to know what I was doing spending the night in that sacred place. I had to hold myself back from popping him in the nose as he probably was the one responsible for locking me in and turning out the lights. He thought the whole thing was very funny, I didn't. But to make-up for the inconvenience, he gave me ten bucks and bought me breakfast, which calmed me down very quickly. I also asked him to write a note explaining what happened so I could present it to my father, which I knew he wouldn't believe anyway, but I thought it was worth a try.

Forty-plus years later, I was at a ballroom dance hall in New Hyde Park, Long Island, New York and I noticed someone doing a Peabody with a girl about twelve inches taller than him. After several sightings, I approached him and asked if he recognized me, as I thought he looked familiar. He said no and we searched our pasts to see if we had something in common. We both came from the same neighborhood in East New York, but he was ten years older than me and was long gone, fighting in WWII, when I lived there. He said in his earlier years he taught printing in upstate New York and that rang a bell. I asked him: "Did you ever work for Appeal Printing?" He replied with a resounding "YES." So there he was, my childhood idol, looking me in the eye and wondering who I was. I told him the warehouse story and he broke out laughing remembering the incident as if it was yesterday. We hugged and mirrored tears in our eyes and spent the rest of the evening going over the history of our lives. I finally asked him if he locked me in the warehouse on purpose or was it an accident. He said he couldn't remember, but there was a mischievous twinkle in his eyes that went along with his reply. We are still the best of friends today and enjoy ballroom dancing in New York in the summer months and Florida in the winter. He married the very tall beautiful gal, Ellie, and they are living happily in both locations. We celebrated his seventy-fifth birthday at the Rainbow Room in Rockefeller Center in Manhattan about ten years ago, and cherish the memory of that evening and our friendship.

My 1936 convertible Ford with a rumble seat in the back, which was still the love-of-my-life, was causing me to spend more time under the hood than in the driver's seat. Plus, I was eighteen, with a driver's license, and the girls I drove around were starting to complain that someone of my stature should own a nicer and more reliable vehicle. Another lesson learned and link added to my character-chain; girls don't really love you, it's the car they love. Taking the hint, I sold my chartreuse baby and bought a shiny black two-year old 1950 Chevrolet Fleetline Deluxe four-door model. It had 90-horsepower @ 3300 RPM and best of all, it had an automatic transmission. It cost $1,000.00. I paid $250.00 down and got my first payment book for a two-year loan. Next link in my character-chain: twenty-four months is a long time to be making payments, especially if you don't have a cash reserve in the bank. But, foolish or not, I again became the most popular guy on the block, as no one had any set of wheels that could compare to my shiny Black Knight, as we can see from the picture of its twin below:

My father never owned a car; his main method of transportation was the elaborate Brooklyn train system. He was flabbergasted that his teenage son could afford such a fine vehicle (which I couldn't). He was angry until I took him and my grandmother for a ride around the neighborhood, with the radio playing Italian music, which got them singing a duet in the back seat of my Knight. From that time on my father assigned me the job of being his chauffeur, transporting him around town doing his errands or just driving around to show-off to his friends what a fine son he must have to be the owner of the shiny Black Knight. My grandmother bribed me with meatball sandwiches so I would take her to her girlfriends' houses, the Italian deli or the chicken market to get recently plucked and beheaded chickens. Her big thrill was having me pick her up after visiting friends and inviting them to come along for a ride in her "rich grandson's" car.

During one of my menial jobs, which included working with my father in the garment industry as a sewing machine operator and an apprentice pattern maker, we moved in with my grandmother Angelina (Tootsie) after the death of my wonderful step-grandfather Peter Messina. We were back to Liberty Avenue, just a couple of blocks from my birthplace. The thought of returning back to square-one on Liberty Avenue in a cold-water-railroad-flat was not to my liking. What I absolutely hated was going down to the basement every morning and filling the coal bucket to get our potbelly and cooking stoves going. So at age 18, I sold my Black Knight and joined the United States Air Force with my good friend Paul Maggio. Not having to make the monthly car payments was a great relief for me and probably one of the reasons that influenced me to join the military. It would be a long time before I bought anything that had time payments; I figured if I didn't have the cash, then I didn't need the item. Another deciding factor was the male-fixtures that hung around the corners of my neighborhood. Since I was a young boy, I remembered teenagers, and even grown men hanging around the corners wasting their time gabbing, whistling at girls passing by and just being annoying in their chatter and appearance. A childhood idol of mine, who was one of the fixtures, got married, and I thought his hanging-around days were over, but after a couple of weeks of marital bliss, he took his place as a fixture at his old location on the street corner. I pictured myself being one of the male-fixtures, and decided that it wasn't what I wanted in my future. The link here in my character-chain was: "Don't go with the flow if the flow isn't going anywhere." Another link that would stay with me for the rest of my life was, "Don't borrow money unless it's absolutely necessary, and if you do, pay it back as soon as possible."

It was the middle of the Korean Conflict and was only a matter of time before I was drafted into the Army for two years. From my National Guard experience, I knew the Army wasn't the place for me, too much physical activity and the possibility of killing people wasn't something I was anxious to do. So I weighed joining the Navy or Air Force for four years. Being cooped up on a ship wasn't very appealing to me either, so the only choice left was enlisting in the United States Air Force, which I thought would probably also be a great way to travel around the world, free of charge, by plane. Although I didn't have a high school education, my typing skills and National Guard experience got me into the Air Force, where I became a communications specialist (teletype, radio, facsimile and the beginning of something called computers). I knew the military service's discipline and regimented life was just what I needed to firm up my character and give me some direction, which I was in desperate need of. I also knew that it would put me in a better place than on the street corners of my neighborhood with my childhood buddies.

My first assignment was at Sampson Air Force Base near the City of Geneva, New York, for three months of basic training, from early October, 1952 to early January, 1953. The base is located in the New York "Snow Belt" and has for its neighbors the City of Rochester (40 miles), Niagara Falls (70 miles), and Seneca Lake in its backyard. The base was formerly a Naval Submarine training center where the lake's deepest depth (600 feet) and length (38 miles) allowed vessels the opportunity to practice in simulated ocean conditions. Seneca is the largest of the glacial Five Finger Lakes, which are, Canandaigua Lake, Honeoye Lake, Seneca Lake, Keuka Lake & Hemlock Lake. The Naval base was converted into an Air Force Training Center during the Korean War. Unlucky me, I got to be stationed at probably one of the coldest places in the United States. When the cold air hit the semi-frozen lake in the winter, the temperature at the base would go down to below zero, which was always followed with icicles forming in my nostrils when we would do our daily outdoor calisthenics.

We were billeted in open barracks (no partitions) with 70 men in each building. Our new home was heated by a coal furnace which blew hot air into the barracks like a wind storm, creating an annoying howling and whistling sound. After being assigned our bunks, a bulky, muscular, buck sergeant (three stripes) named Fargo, began to instruct us in how to properly make a military bed. By the expressions on my fellow recruits' faces, I could see that they agreed with me; "Are we children? We know how to make a bed." But Sgt. Fargo had other ideas. He said, "There is only one way to make a bunk, and that is the military way. If you don't make it right, it's 50 pushups, and if you don't make it right three times, then no blankets or sheets on the bunks for the next day." He got everyone's attention and we learned how to make hospital corners and tight sheets and blankets in a very short period of time. To pass the tightness test, he would bounce a quarter in the center of the blanket, if it didn't bounce six inches, you failed the test. That event was the beginning of what we in the military called "Chicken Sh…" The popular term means, "Expending an inordinate amount of time doing 'minutia manure' tasks for the benefit of no one in particular." After settling in, we were brought to the supply room for uniform fittings. We were asked: "What size shirt? What size jacket and pants? What size hat and what size shoes?" After all that guess work, when we put our uniforms on we looked like a bunch of misfits. The only thing that fit properly was something called "Long Johns," which were thermal underwear that seem to immediately attach to one's skin. Our crowning moment was at the barber shop. I was asked how I would prefer my curly-red-hair trimmed. I said "Long in the back and short in the front." I didn't get the last word out of my mouth before he removed all the hair from my head except for about ½ an inch, which made my nose seem that it was a transplant from Cyrano de Bergerac's face.

I was called into Sgt. Fargo's private room that was at the head of our barracks, and while standing at strict attention I said: "Sir, Airman Michael Bivona, serial number 21909846 reporting as ordered." Much to my surprise, he asked me to sit down and produced my military file. He pointed out that I had served in the Army National Guard, and due to my former military training he was considering me as an assistant drill instructor. He told me to think it over and get back to him that evening before "Lights out," which was 9 PM.

To add icing on the cake, he mentioned I would be getting my private stripe and an increase in pay right away, instead of after basic training in three months. It was one of the first major military decisions that crossed my path and I was tempted to take on the job. But, my experience in the National Guard was not a pleasant one when it came to giving orders to other soldiers; I was always uncomfortable, and especially ill-at-ease with the angry responses that invariably resulted when the men didn't like the directives, which was usually all the time. I was also unhappy that there was a possibility that I could remain behind after boot camp and become a permanent assistant instructor, which the Air Force was in dire need, as most of the new recruits had no prior military experience. Other important considerations were that I would be separated from the two friends that I enlisted with and would also have to give them orders. After some serious thought, I decided not to accept the position, so I didn't visit Sgt. Fargo that evening.

Another airman was assigned the assistant's job. I thought the whole matter was behind me, but for some unexplained reason, out of the 70 men in the building, I was assigned to "Coal Duty," which meant getting up at 5:30 AM, a half an hour before reveille (bugle call) and shoveling obnoxious smelling coal into the furnace so that the barracks would be comfy for my fellow airmen when they woke up to take their cold showers. Another lesson learned and an important link was added to my character-chain. I should have met with Sgt. Fargo and told him my reasons for not wanting the position instead of avoiding the issue by letting it go-away unresolved. The upside was that I was already an old hand at shoveling coal into stoves; unfortunately it brought back the same dreadful feelings I had when maintaining my grandmother's coal stoves. . . . UGH!!

The three months couldn't go by fast enough. As fall turned into winter, the weather became intolerably cold, especially when we had to camp outdoors for days at a time. The fierce winds would hit the partially frozen lake and blanket us with ice-mists that would chill my body with no escape or relief. But, like all good soldiers, we all managed to survive and lived to tell our family and friends how we almost froze to death. The daily routine for everyone but me, was to "rise and shine" to the sounds of the bugle coming through the loudspeakers, at 6 AM, (I was up a half hour earlier). We had to fall in line at 6:30 AM, then march and run in the cold morning air until icicles formed under my wool mask and around my eyebrows and into my nose; it felt like the ice in my nose was going to puncture my brain. We drilled for an hour and then trotted at quickstep straight to the "Chow Line" and some much needed heat. Breakfast became the most important event of the day; after an hour of drilling and nearly freezing our butts off, the hot coffee, bacon and eggs, biscuits and more hot coffee was something everyone looked forward to as a reward for doing our jobs well. After breakfast we attended classes learning the Code of Military Conduct, how to survive in hostile situations, how to be a gentleman, how to brush our teeth (eight strokes in each area), and how to have proper table manners. We also learned how to strip our M2 Carbines and .45 Caliber Pistols. It was hard to believe that over 15,000 Airmen were going through the same training that we were at the same time. I became fascinated at the organizational skills that were required to successfully control such a large number of people. My curiosity continued during and after basic training, and whenever a chance would present itself, I would volunteer to help out with administrative and organizational duties. The links in my character-chain were growing as I added more important links: "Success requires teamwork; great successes, requires lots of teamwork." I also learned that "The early bird catches the worm, but it's the early worm that the bird catches." I certainly was the early bird and worm in my outfit; I was up one-half-an-hour before everyone else, in freezing weather with very little heat, until I started shoveling the black coal into the furnace.

A most memorable experience took place after a couple of months in boot camp. Members of our family were allowed to join us and spend a day at the camp enjoying the facilities, including eating the great food in the Mess Hall. My father, Luciano Joseph, came to visit. He had to take a railroad train for over 300 miles, carrying a large pot of cheese ravioli, and a picnic basket of meatballs, chicken and sausages that my grandmother Angelina made for the special visit. Till this day, I think miraculously, that there was still some heat remaining in the pot when it arrived. Many of my roommates decided to forgo chow in the Mess Hall and share the cuisine with us right in our barracks. Mysteriously, a bottle of wine and Italian bread appeared and was added to my father's delicious picnic spread, which we devoured in short order with lots of OOHS and AHHS coming from the half-a-dozen delighted diners. After our late lunch we went to the cafeteria where my buddies treated my father and me to coffee and dessert. Some of my buddies adopted my father and gave him the nickname of "Papa Joe." Another link was added that day to my character-chain: "My father was a pretty nice guy and he liked me." This was a great awakening for a young, rebellious lad. From that time on, whatever differences, real or imaginary that I had with my father seemed to fade away. A picture of my father, Luciano Joseph Bivona; my grandmother Angelina Bivona Messina; my sister Mae Bivona (eventually Mae Bivona Curti) and moi follows:

I was 21-years-old and still in the military, stationed at Mitchel Field in Hempstead, New York, just twenty miles from my home on Montauk

Avenue in Brooklyn, when the picture was taken; Papa Joe was 61-years old, my precious grandmother Angelina was 80-years old, and my sister Mae was 25. The yellow canary in the background was ageless.

Another memorable event in boot camp was my first weekend-pass. The closest city was Geneva, which was a short distance from our base, but the city of choice for most of the men was Rochester, which was only a little over one hour away. It was rumored that their USO Club had beautiful female volunteer hostesses who were willing to talk and dance with soldiers. It was over two months since we had any contact with women, so we were all anxious to get on the bus and see what the City of Rochester and its environs had to offer. The USO (United Service Organization) was founded in 1941 and was a "Home away from home" for American servicemen around the world. It gave them a quiet place to talk, write a letter home, get a free cup of coffee and a snack, attend socials and dances, and enjoy the entertainment of many famous Hollywood celebrities who volunteered their time for the benefit of the servicemen and women in the military. The organization was sponsored by the Salvation Army, Young Men's Christian Association (YMCA), Young Women's Christian Association (YWCA), National Catholic Community Service, National Travelers Aid Association and the National Jewish Welfare Board. These not-for-profit organizations combined their efforts to raise money to support the everyday activities that benefited millions of servicemen and women during WWII. It was disbanded after the Second World War and reestablished in 1950 during the Korean Conflict. It served 3.5 million men during my first year in the Air Force in 1952. We were all very anxious to go to the USO canteen in Rochester because of all the good things we had heard about their treatment of GIs.

Getting to Rochester was easy; making it even more enjoyable was the fact that the USO was right at the train terminal. We were treated to coffee and cake when we entered the large hall by pretty young girls that welcomed us as if we were family members returning home from the war. The first order of the day was to find a place to sleep for two nights. We were given a list of nearby hotels, motels and boarding houses that had discount prices for men in the military. I and my two buddies, Frank and Johnny chose a nearby hotel that allowed the three of us to share a room at a very reasonable price. The small L-shaped room had two single beds and a pull-out couch. After over two months of sharing an open barracks with seventy other soldiers who made the most unimaginable sounds in their sleep, the hotel room seemed like a quiet prince's palace.

It was in the middle of December and near the Xmas holidays, so the city was decorated for the festive religious occasion. Everyone we met was in the spirit of the holiday, which resulted in our getting free drinks and many free meals in the restaurants and bars we visited. Especially nice was the dance at the USO Club. It was also decorated for the occasion; a large 12-foot local Xmas tree was harvested; its pine fragrance filled the hall bringing rushing memories of the many days spent at my grandmother Tootsie's house decorating her freshly cut trees and inhaling the same aroma that was in abundance in the hall and around the neighborhoods of Rochester. We were invited to a Holiday Dance on Saturday night at the USO Club, which gave us an opportunity to dress for the first time in our formal blue uniforms, wearing our handsomely boxed visor hats and mirror shined black dress shoes, minus our winter long johns. We were welcomed by the pretty volunteers whose numbers magically grew to match the amount of men present at the party; approximately 100 pretty shiny faces were there to share in the holiday spirit. We spent the night dancing; talking, spiking our soft drinks and listening to the girls tell us how much they appreciated our being in the military and our willingness to put our lives at risk for their benefit. Wow!! I never thought about it that way; I could actually get killed in this growing-up process. Another number of links in my character-chain: "When you volunteer for something, make sure you weigh the downside before being magnetized by the hype that draws you into the arena." I also learned that volunteering, as all the pretty girls did, not only brought pleasure to others but certainly had its own rewards, which was evident on the smiling, beaming faces of the young girls. When the weekend was over, I etched the incredible experience in my mind. I met beautiful girls who were willing to devote their spare time for the benefit of servicemen that they didn't know. We also met some of the friendly people of Rochester who invited many of us to share their homes and dinner tables Christmas day; it's not surprising that today the city is considered one of the ten best places to live in the United States. I thought at that time that living there in the future wouldn't be such a bad idea.

We returned to Sampson AFB and continued our drilling and studies, and in the blink of an eye our basic training was over. On graduation day, we joined hundreds of other flights in formations on the parade field and marched past the officers' grandstand, saluting, while a dozen F84 Thunder Fighting Jets (training planes) flew overhead leaving their thunderous noise and jet streams in the sky as they passed. What a feeling; I had my new stripe on my sleeves (Private First Class), I was part of a group of men that successfully completed three grueling months of boot camp, and part of the best flying organization in the world. I was proud to have finally finished something in my life that was important and useful to me, my fellow Airmen, and to my country. A big bonus for graduating was that we were leaving the freezing weather behind, but I did hold onto my winter long johns that served me so well, just in case my next tour of duty was in Alaska.

There was a new program instituted in the Air Force that allowed men that were not circumcised the opportunity to become a "clipped" person, it was supposed to make life healthier and more fun. It was a voluntary event and I was one of many airmen that decided it was a good idea. So at age 18, I had a Jewish christening and probably became the first Italian-American in East New York to be circumcised. Years later the procedure became a common event in hospitals around the country.

My next assignment was at Francis E. Warren Air Force Base, in Cheyenne, Wyoming, which was about 1,500 miles away. Our mode of transportation was a C-54 Skymaster, a military transport plane that dated back to WWII and was developed from the four-engine prop Douglas DC-4 Airliner. A picture of the beautiful lady is below:

About 50 Airmen from the graduating flights, who were going to Francis E. Warren AFB, were gathered together at the airstrip and nervously waited boarding the shiny lady. I was the only one from my flight going to Cheyenne and felt uneasy about leaving my buddies behind. I was scared and excited at the same time. It was my first experience with air-flight and couldn't wait for the thrill of taking-off and getting airborne, just as I saw so many of my movie war heroes like John Wayne and Errol Flynn do in their wartime movie roles. We boarded the aircraft and sat side by side along the length of the plane. Shoulder to shoulder, teenagers trying to act grownup, but scared as hell, especially when the flight sergeant told us that there was a parachute under each position. His only instruction for their use was "Put this thing on, buckle the front, tie the top and bottom and then jump out this door; after you exit, count to ten and pull this ring," that was the end of our visual and verbal instructions.

The four engines roared and in short order we were airborne. We flew over Michigan, Illinois, Iowa and Nebraska. Nebraska—Nebraska—Nebraska—the sound of a state that I will never forget. I call it a sound instead of a name because after hearing it in so many sentences the words got garbled. "We have developed ice on our wings and we are going to have to land in Nebraska, put on your parachutes and make ready in case we have to bail out." I thought, "Is this guy nuts?" I didn't know the first thing about jumping out of a plane, no less in freezing weather. We scrambled for our chutes and somehow got them on and checked by our brilliant flight sergeant. He remarked: "Don't worry men; the worst thing that can happen is you freeze up and remain in the sky or maybe come down as a snowflake." He then said: "If we don't make a crash landing in the cornfields, we will be landing at Offutt Air Force Base in Omaha, Nebraska in approximately ten-minutes." There wasn't a peep from the fifty grownup soldiers, only stillness, the only thing that could be heard was the silence and my heart beating through the inside of my ears. The brilliant one then said: "Hold on men, we are going to be losing altitude pretty fast, so if you have to pee, do it now, but don't leave your seats."

We landed and due to the additional weight from the icing, the plane thudded and bounced along the runway until it came to a stop. The runway was lit with torches to light our way and to probably melt some of the snow from its surface. When the C-54 finally ended its flight and shut off its huge noisy engines, the silence in the plane became even louder. It seemed that everyone was in suspended animation, we were frozen in place and didn't dare move for fear of waking up and finding out we were dead. We finally thawed-out, removed the parachute armor, grabbed our duffle bags and got the hell off the shiny lady. Looking back at the plane, I could actually see icicles hanging from the wings and caked on the fuselage. Our plane was dwarfed by SAC's humongous fighting machines; B-29s, B-50s and an assortment of other sophisticated flying equipment. Our unexpected location was Offutt Air Force Base, headquarters for the Strategic Air Command (SAC) and the very place where the first two bombers, the B-29 Superfortresses, Enola Gay and Bockscar, that dropped atomic bombs on Hiroshima and Nagasaki, Japan, were built.

Two busses were waiting for us. We rushed in quickstep to board and were on our way to Wyoming in short order. The whole maneuver was so efficient that I got the feeling that the routine must have been done many times before. It would have been nice if our brilliant flight sergeant mentioned that what was happening was routine. It certainly would have taken the pressure off the fifty teenager-grownups. We drove the remaining part of the day and the following night, making some necessary pit stops, before arriving at Francis E. Warren AFB late the next morning. How do I begin to explain the shock of getting off the bus and walking into the severe cold air? The temperatures we left behind in Sampson AFB were springtime by comparison. The shock of zero degree temperature, the mounds of snow along the roads and paths, and the ferocious wind pounding at me like a sledge hammer, made me wish that I was back home in Brooklyn in our cold-water-flat. The elevation of the base is over 6,000 feet which accounts for the fact that the Cheyenne, Wyoming location is one of the, if not the, windiest places in the United States. When the first fort was built on that location in the late 1800s, the buildings were built in a triangular shape with the main point facing the prevailing winds to reduce damage to the structures. Talk about going from the frying pan into the fire (pun intended), the base had to be the coldest place I could ever imagine and is probably why I love staying in Florida for six winter months every year in my senior days. Another link was added to my character-chain: "No matter how bad you think things are, they can always get worse; so when complaining, always try to find a bright side of the situation and concentrate on it." Well, there was some redeeming information that our new flight sergeant lectured us about. He pointed out where we would be spending most of our classroom days learning our new communication skills; thank God the classes were indoors. He also told us that reveille was at 7 AM, and that our classes started an hour later with no outside marching, running or drills required before or after breakfast. He escorted us through the valley of snow to our pre-WWI barracks; it was identical to the one we left behind at Sampson AFB. He then gave us some much needed good news; our classes didn't start for another week because most of the staff was still on holiday vacations, so after some orientation that afternoon, we had the rest of the day to ourselves, including going into the city of Cheyenne, which was only a couple of miles away and could be reached by shuttle busses that ran every half-an-hour till 10 PM when everyone was expected to be back in their barracks. After orientation he called me aside to inform me that I was the barracks' Fire Marshal being that I had experience with coal furnaces. I was trapped again, the big difference was that I didn't have to shovel any coal; my job was to make sure that it was shoveled by someone else. A picture of me and three of my buddies leaning against a snow bank outside our barracks follows:

I can't express the feeling of euphoria and gratitude that I felt when hearing the bugle-call at 7 AM, waking up and then deliberately going back to sleep with no fear of retribution. It was the first time in over three months that I actually had time to myself with nothing to do. So me and my buddies, Tim and Phil went to a late breakfast at 9 AM, and spent the rest of the day exploring the base by shuttle bus. One of the strange things about the base was it had a very minor dirt airstrip. Considering that it was a large Air Force Base, there was very little air traffic at the facility. Most of the major air traffic was at the Air National Guard Base that was in the area. Another strange sight was a network of wires or ropes with pulleys that went from each barrack to the Mess Hall. In inclement weather, before paths could be cleared, food would be transported from the kitchen by pulley systems to the individual buildings. Seeing that procedure in operation was like imagining a mother with multiple umbilical cords feeding her children. The base was used primarily as a training center and was the proud host of the United States ICBM missile headquarters.

Our bus driver freely gave us some information about the base: "Francis E. Warren AFB was named after Wyoming's first governor, who also served as a U.S. Senator for 37 years. At age 19 he was the winner of the Medal of Honor for heroism during the Civil War. He was also the father-in-law of the General of the Armies during WWI, 'Black Jack' Pershing, who as a captain was stationed at the fort prior to it becoming an air base. Other well-known figures stationed there were General Billy Mitchell (the 'Father of the Air Force'), General Mark Clark who served in WWI, WWII and was the Supreme UN Commander in the Korean War and eventually the signer of the final cease fire document ending that conflict. Some rather amusing information was that entertainers Neil Diamond and Chris LeDoux grew up on that base."

I noticed a civilian walking along the white snow background wearing royal blue pants. There was only one person in the world that I knew who owned such a pair of pistol pocket, royal blue tapered cuffed pants; it had to be my hometown buddy Paul Maggio. We got off the bus and ran after him, lo and behold, it was him. What a small world, I hadn't seen him since we signed up together back in Brooklyn. He was called up before me and was sent to Lackland Air Force Base in San Antonio, Texas for motor pool management. He was stationed at our base for further training and was to be reassigned at a later date. What a lucky break, we now had someone who could tell us where the best places were for entertainment. He took us to the PX (Post Exchange) and introduced us to the greatest little coffee shop in the world that boasted having the best cream filled donuts on our planet. He told us that the nearest civilized city was Cheyenne, the capital of Wyoming with a population of about 30,000 residents. It was probably the smallest-big-city in the U.S. by population. We made plans with him to visit the most popular place in the town, the "Trolley Car Diner," the next morning for their special breakfast. And special it was; stacks of hotcakes, mounds of bacon and for a morning dessert, "apple pie a la mode." I didn't know such a treat existed as pie with vanilla ice cream on top. Till this day it's still one of my favorite desserts, vanilla ice cream on apple or blueberry pie. Well that was the extent of what was exciting in the smallest-big-city in the U.S. Paul told us that for real entertainment and lots of girls we would have to travel 100 miles to Denver, Colorado. He showed us around the town (Cheyenne was really too small to call a city). There was a movie house, a couple of diners, some retail stores, and lots of cowboys riding horses. It seemed that it was easier to get around locally by horse than by motorized vehicles. I was glad to be in horse country and made a mental note to do some horseback riding; weather permitting.

After goofing off for almost a week in town visiting the movies, some local bars and just hanging around the Service Men's Club on the base while trying to keep warm, our classes began. The essence of our training was to study Morse Code, teletype operations including code identification, typing, telegraph, and facsimile operations. Our training would be for four months and then we would be assigned to Air Force networks throughout the world. My typing skills, which I developed in junior high school under the tutelage of the beautiful Miss Baily, would help me through the grueling class work and practice sessions. Spending four months in a classroom without cutting class was a new experience for me, and I enjoyed every bit of it. Although learning Morse Code and teletype code was difficult, most of the guys had considerably more trouble learning how to type; except for me, thanks to Miss Baily's endowments. It took lots of studying and practice to master the operation of telegraph transmission in Morse Code, but the more difficult task was learning to operate, read and transmit teletype information using a ¾ inch perforated tape system. A copy of the International Morse Code follows:

A copy of the more complicated International Teletype Code follows:

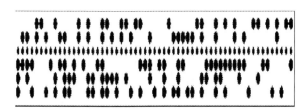

The perforated tape is approximately ¾s of an inch wide and consists of one to five perforations per letter. The following is my name and address, Michael Bivona 9 Broadley Ct Melville, NY United States. The first three vertical perforations is an M the second an I and so on:

Studying was something that I never did in earnest before, but the classes in communication were fascinating, I couldn't believe how absorbed I became in learning my new job as a Communication Specialist. I actually had a titled job and began to feel very much like a grownup.

Getting to Denver, Colorado was not an easy task, we either had to take a bus or train, and both had very infrequent and unreliable schedules, and were very expensive. So, three of my buddies and I (the ones in the above snow bank picture) decided to buy a twelve year old 1941 Chevrolet Sedan for $200.00. A picture of a like-new Chevy follows; it's a far cry from the one we bought which was green and pretty dented with lots of rust spots:

With the addition of the beat-up Chevy in our lives, we gained an incredible amount of freedom in choosing where we should travel. We developed a system where each of us had a choice as to what destination our new baby would transport us. A lesson that I learned long ago proved to still hold true; "If you have wheels, girls will be at your heels." As we traveled around the military base in our new wheels, the WAFs (Women in the Air Force) all of a sudden noticed that we existed. We were so busy dating the girls on the base that getting to Denver was getting difficult. We developed a fair system of using the Chevy so that we all had equal turns. Each of us got a chance to use the car from Monday through Thursday. Fridays, Saturdays and Sundays we had to double up and any dating had to be in pairs. The exceptions were when we visited Denver or decided to go someplace as a group. The system worked fairly well, considering the amount of WAFs on the base that discovered how handsome we were when we were behind the wheel of our green jalopy. Another link was added to my character-chain: "Having partners can make life easier, allow you to get things you can't afford on your own, and can help with solutions to problems, as many heads are better than one."

Our classes were Monday through Friday from 8 AM till 4 PM, so we had lots of time to study, with weekends off to travel and see the countryside. Due to the severe weather conditions that time of year, we had to be very careful in deciding our travel plans as unexpected blizzards were always waiting to cause grief to inexperienced travelers, which we were. So we spent lots of time on the base at the Service Men's Club socializing with the gracious WAFs and sometimes driving them around town, visiting the movie house and the ever popular "Trolley Car Diner." When weather conditions were favorable, we would drive for two hours to Denver, Colorado to visit dancehalls and get to know civilian cowgirls that seemed to be a part of the fixtures at the halls. Denver is the Capital of Colorado and had a population at that time of over 200,000 people and is probably one of the most beautiful cosmopolitan small-town-places in the United States. Although it was a large city, its neighborhoods had a small town feeling. The people were very hospitable and treated servicemen with respect. It is surrounded by the Rocky Mountains to the west and the High Plains to the east. Considering that it's only a couple of hours away from Cheyenne, the climate is a lot different. It boasts as having over 300 days of sunshine a year, with semi-arid climate resulting in mild temperatures and moderate humidity. It has four distinct seasons and although it can get heavy amounts of snow, the abundance of sunshine makes it a comfortable place to visit, and absolutely a great place to live; even in the months we were there (January through April).

Our favorite dancehall in Denver was the Palomino Club. It was a large country western hall that had the greatest music in the area for dancing, mixing Country music with Swing and Cha-Chas. The 3,000 square foot palace was filled with dancers from end to end, but had a large dance floor which allowed us plenty of room to express ourselves and socialize with the cowgirls. There were lots of pretty women dressed in western outfits of every imaginable color, with high heeled boots to match, and they were more than happy to talk and dance with servicemen. There was also an electric bull on the premises. For two-dollars anyone, male or female, could try their luck on the rocking-vibrating-monster with big horns. I and my buddies each tried to ride it to show that we were macho guys, but it didn't work, we were thrown in a matter of seconds. The disengagement was called "up and out," and entitled us to a large glass of tap beer and a complimentary soft cushion to ease our pain. For some reason the girls got friendlier when we were thrown from the big bull and showed our less masculine side.

We visited Denver about six times during our stay. One memorable occasion was on our trip back from Denver to Cheyenne. We got caught in a snow storm and our usual two hour trip took us six hours with the possibility of our getting snowbound and possibly freezing to death. We had to ride with the left tires on the highway and the right on the dirt road to get traction. We also filled our trunk with snow to add weight to the vehicle. It was the scariest experience for all of us up until that point in our young lives. That was the last winter trip we made to Denver; we waited till early spring before returning to the magnificent city to visit the many friends we made on our previous visits. The city in springtime miraculously changed from a winter snowbound sunny wonderland into a spring flowerbound sunny paradise. Some of my most pleasant daytime activities were walking around the city enjoying the warm weather, good restaurants, the abundance of flowers hanging from street posts and doorways, and the friendly smiling faces of the locals. I made a mental note that the beautiful city would probably be another nice place for me to live if future events allowed.

Attending class was very much like holding down a civilian job, as a matter of fact our instructor was a female civilian. One of the major differences between a regular job and our military training was that in civilian life an alarm clock woke you in the morning versus the military's bugle call announcing reveille. A picture of a WAF sounding the morning call follows; she was one of the many young girls training at our base at the same time we were:

A/2C Frances E. Courtney
furnished the bugle calls of
taps and reveille for the
3452nd Student Squadron
(WAF) at Francis E. Warren
Air Force Base in 1953

Not everyone passed the Communication Specialist course: about ten percent of the class was reassigned to other duties as they couldn't pass the exams that were required to complete the program. In our last week of training I came down with pneumonia. I spent two weeks at the base hospital eating lots of bacon (a sure cure in those days), and other fatty foods to line my lungs and protect them from the cold temperatures. A sure cure for pneumonia in those days was to eat lots of greasy foods, keeping windows closed to keep cool air from coming into the room, and lots of rest. How little we knew. Because of my rest period, my group shipped out two weeks before I did.

They all went home on furlough before leaving for Oakland California and then overseas where they hopefully would help bring the Korean War to a speedy conclusion. The upside for me was that in addition to eating lots of bacon, ham, and eggs, I was able to see springtime come alive in Cheyenne. The dismal snowbound city turned into a green snowless massive pasture, with grass, flowers and horses visible in every direction.

One of the biggest and most popular rodeos in the world is Cheyenne's Frontier Days, which is held in July. The show I attended was a practice and elimination competition. I wore a cowboy hat, dungarees, high cowboy boots and a red bandana around my neck. You couldn't tell me from the natives; I fit right in with the loud roaring crowds. The beatings that the young riders took while riding bulls, calves and horses defy description. Many a young lad was taken from the field on stretchers with broken arms, legs and necks. The more interesting part of the event was the horse shows where cowboys showed how smart their horses were by having them bow, walk backwards, walk sideways, count to ten, and reining up on command while neighing. There were also spectacular shows by cowgirls that were similar to exhibitions at football games. The cowgirls danced, twirled their batons, made human pyramids and spelled out the name of their favorite state, Wyoming. Their routines were more entertaining than the cowboy riders, and a lot less dangerous.

Frontier Days, which is the last week of July, draws people from around the globe to witness the longest running rodeo in the world. The first show started in 1897 and has developed into a massive carnival type event with rides for children that could compete with some of Coney Island's play toys of olden days. Some other attractions are permanent like the "Old West Museum" that follows the history of the Wild West from early frontier days to present times, and a "Wild Horse Gulch" that consists of merchants who easily satisfied everyone's shopping desires, and is serviced by period costumed cowboys and girls imitating Wild Bill Cody, Buffalo Bill, Wyatt Earp and Annie Oakley. Also featured is the "Buckin' A Saloon" where folks can kick up their heels and dance till the wee hours of the morning, while enjoying an amazing variety of beer and other alcoholic concoctions. Also on site is the permanent "Indian Village" that brings the visitors into a replica camp and allows them to smoke peace pipes with the natives. Last but not least is "The Oasis," a food court equal to any in the country. The rodeo and shows are all located in Frontier Park which is laid out to safely control the over 300,000 people that attend the week long festivities. It's amusing to read the "Code of Conduct" pamphlets that are circulated throughout the city prior to the rodeo. Some of the civic violations that will result in being ejected from the park and possibly being arrested are: drunk and disorderly conduct, fighting or challenging others to fight, disturbing other guest's enjoyment of the events, throwing, tossing or discharging any objects, including weapons. From the list of rules, one would say that the Wild West is still alive and well. A copy of a Frontier Day's photo follows:

I was the only one left in my barracks for a week until it was time to leave. My friend Paul Maggio and I decided to do a little horseback riding just as we did in the good old days in Brooklyn. We rented two beautiful mares, mine was a brown and white Pinto; his was a charcoal lady with a bright white mane and tail. We had an hour to ride and reminisce about the times we spent at the horse stables with our teenage friends. We walked the girls for a while and then got daring; we decided to do a little trotting and then cantering. When we got the feel of the ladies, we galloped full speed to see which horse was the fastest. Little did we know that a sheriff was keeping an eye on us through his binoculars. He came after us blowing a hand held horn. We slowed down and waited for him to approach, I thought he was a bandit and was going to start shooting. Flashing his big badge he told us that we were breaking the law. Paul said: "What Law?" He said: "You boys were galloping the horses and anything over a canter is downright cruel to animals and could get them pneumonia, so you broke the law." He wrote us both five-dollar speeding tickets and told us to get the horses back to the stables before they caught their death from sweating so much. Well, that was a new experience for us. I'm sure that in our lifetimes we will get tickets for speeding cars but I didn't think we would ever again get a citation for speeding horses.

The next day Paul drove me to the Cheyenne Train Station, in the jalopy that we sold him, to begin a two weeks furlough in my Brooklyn, N.Y. coal-water-flat home on Liberty Avenue. I hadn't seen my family in over seven months, except for Papa Joe's short visit to Sampson AFB. Keep in mind that telephones were not readily available in those days, so I didn't have a chance to speak to anyone since I left home in October. As a matter of fact, if I did call my father, I would have to call the candy store across the street from our home and plead with them to get my father to cross over, if he happened to be available. So having just turned 19, I took my first overnight railroad train ride from Cheyenne, Wyoming to Pennsylvania Station in Manhattan, New York. The ride was not only boring, but there were times that I was the only person in the passenger car for hours. I slept sitting up or stretched out across two seats, in either case, the ride was long, and my attempt at sleeping comfortably was out of the question as in addition to the awkward sleeping positions I found myself in, the train would occasionally jerk when making turns or slowing down, waking me from my light sleep. It took three uncomfortable days of listening to the sounds of the endless monotonous clattering of the train's wheels running over the railroad tracks before I reached my destination in New York City. I took the Eighth Avenue Subway to the Cleveland Street station on Pitkin Avenue. Exiting the subway and onto the street carrying my 50-pound duffle bag made me look and feel out of place. My uniform certainly made me a stranger in a civilian neighborhood as I walked the two city blocks to Liberty Avenue, returning peoples' waves and nodding recognition of their friendly greetings.

My father and grandmother made a dinner party and invited my family over to our flat to celebrate my return and also to wish me luck on my new journey. A birthday cake appeared and everyone sang the world's most popular song. I was entering the last teenage year of my life, 19, thereafter, I would no longer carry that teenager moniker around; I would be referred to after the end of the year as a grownup, finally. No one in my family owned a car, so I had a choice of walking or taking a subway train to visit friends in my old neighborhood on Pitkin Avenue. It was early summer so walking the half-a-mile was my choice for traveling. I walked on Liberty Avenue past my birth-home and the playground where my mother used to carefully push the children's swing while I screamed with delight. Across the street from my first home was Gilibertes' Drug Store where my mother, to earn extra money during the Depression, cared for the owner's elderly parent. I continued walking on the avenue past my second home on the same side of the street, over Mr. Bono's two-family building which had a social club on the street level. I reminisced being hit by a car when I was five-years-old and being rushed to the hospital in critical condition for a month long stay, it happened right outside of the building that I lived in at that time. Turning left at the corner, which was Hendrix Street, and walking one block brought me to Glenmore Avenue, the street where my brother Vic and sister-in-law Rose lived. Continuing for another block on Hendrix Street put me in front of the house on Pitkin Avenue where I spent most of my teenage years. Making a right turn on Pitkin Avenue to the end of the street, put me in front of Brandt's Ice Cream Parlor where my friends and I spent lots of time listening to juke box music while sucking down ice cream sodas and eating banana splits. Not only was the ice cream parlor still there, but my buddies were still hanging around in front of it and on the street corner near the subway station. All were still part of the scenery, fixtures for life, trapped by their environment and the mental conditioning that convinced them that they were at home with their lot. I spent a couple of hours chatting with my friends while devouring a delicious Brooklyn egg-cream, which by the way doesn't have any eggs in it, just chocolate syrup, some milk and a shot of seltzer. Saying my goodbyes, I quickly walked away from the whole scene that had become distasteful to me, and hurried back to my cold-water-flat and my father and grandmother Tootsie on Liberty Avenue.

My travel orders only stated that my destination was Oakland Naval Station in Oakland, California. After visiting and alternating dinners with my wonderful family, I left for my new assignment. I could either fly or take a train for the almost 3,000 miles to California. Since my last flying experience, airplanes were not my choice of transportation. So, my father and I headed for Pennsylvania Station in New York City, where I boarded a locomotive train for California, hoping that it would be a more pleasant journey than my previous long distance train ride. After boarding, I looked back and saw my father waving; he had tears in his eyes complemented by an enormous smile on his face. I could never quite figure out which was the dominant reaction. Did the tears say he was sorry to see me leaving? Was the smile a happy one reflecting how pleased he was to get rid of me? Or maybe it was a little bit of both!! The trip was a tedious one, four days and three nights sitting and sleeping on seats that semi reclined. The only salvation was the sandwiches that my grandmother Tootsie made consisting of eggplant, meatballs, and potatoes and eggs. As we got closer to California, the train filled with other servicemen which made the ride a little more tolerable as I was able to discuss military matters with them and how we were all looking forward to going overseas. Another major link to my character-chain developed: "Never take long train rides if there is an alternative, unless totally necessary."

I joined my fellow communication specialists who were still waiting to get their overseas assignments and were just passing the time of day until the information became available. Our orders finally came, we had to wait for another week and then it was off to Korea, which is where we figured we were going all along. We were able to get weekend passes and my Chevy buddies and I headed for San Francisco which was on the opposite side of the San Francisco-Oakland Bridge. We took a shuttle bus across the enormous two-leveled suspension bridge to our destination. When in a new city the best place for servicemen to get oriented is usually the USO, so that is where we headed. It was very similar to the one in Rochester, N.Y., with a large open area for dancing and socializing, and friendly hostesses to meet and assist servicemen. Our first concern was where we could find inexpensive lodging. A pretty volunteer named Guinevere gave us some choices, but recommended one that was near Fishermen's Wharf that had lots of places for us to dine and hang out. So we took a Cable Car to the pier area. I couldn't figure out what the fuss was about San Francisco's Cable Cars, everyone told me not to miss a ride on the special cars. The only difference between them and the trolley cars we had on Liberty Avenue in Brooklyn was that they were painted bright red and ours were dull yellow and a mixture of other nondescript colors. On the way to the pier area we passed the foot of the Golden Gate Bridge. The sun reflecting off of the huge single leveled structure actually made the bridge look as if it were painted gold. It's actually painted orange; the name of the structure is in honor of the mid-eighteen hundreds Gold Rush and mining eras. I thought that the San Francisco-Oakland Bridge (Bay

Bridge) was a more significant structure. It has two levels and seemed to travel a longer distance than the Golden Gate Bridge. We also passed the fabled Chinatown neighborhood that is home to the largest group of Chinese people outside of Asia. The change in scenery from the traditional American cut-out houses lined up alongside each other, to the colorful oriental homes and shops, made me feel that we left our homeland and had entered a foreign country. The green Dragon Gate that welcomes guests was not only a work of art in its formation and oriental design, but seemed to relay a message that the people abiding within were proud of their accomplishments and of who they were. We located the hotel that the hostess recommended and were directed to a nice suite with two beds and two pull out bunks, which was far superior to the open barracks' sleeping facilities that we had at the Naval Station. What was especially nice was an 18-inch black and white television set that required 10-cents for an hours use.

The weekend went by fast with our eating at restaurants like the Pompeii and Alioto for great Italian food, we also enjoyed the delicious Dungeness Crabs that were in abundance along the wharf-side bistros. Fishermen's Wharf gets its neighborhood character from the city's early days during the Gold Rush when Italian immigrant fishermen settled the area and netted for Dungeness Crabs. Today it's still home to an active fishing fleet with colorful boats lining and adding character and charm to the wharf area. We also did lots of bar-hopping and carousing with the local ladies. But, as all good things must come to an end, when our time expired, we packed our bags and headed back to the Naval Base in Oakland.

A Robert Burns quote states: "The best laid plans of mice and men go-Gang aft agley." Well, my buddies left for Korea and I found myself at the naval hospital having my appendix removed. Either I ate too much meatloaf at the Mess Hall or the Dungeness Crabs decided to get even with me for devouring so many of their kind. Whatever, I spent the next two weeks in the hospital and had to wait another two weeks before I received my travel orders. Evidently my position was filled in Korea and my new assignment was Nagoya, Japan for further reassignment. I was on my own again, all my buddies from boot camp and from communication school were scattered all over the world at their permanent posts. I didn't have the faintest idea where my permanent assignment would be. It wasn't long before I received my shipping orders. Being that I was in the Air Force you would think that my next mode of transportation would be by plane, but that's not the way the military works. Lucky me, I would get to spend the next two weeks aboard the USS General J. C. Breckinridge troop ship with over 5,000 Army and Marine soldiers, I was one of the few airmen on the ship, which made me stand out like a sore thumb. The Army and Marine uniforms were brownish, mine was blue, UGH!! To get an idea of how crowded the ship was I'll compare it to the Jewel of the Sea cruise ship which I recently had the pleasure of sailing on to the Baltic Countries of Finland, Norway, Sweden, Estonia and Russia. The ship is 1,100 feet long and accommodates approximately 3,600 passengers and over 1,000 crew members. The troop ship was a little more than half that length and had almost twice as many passengers as the modern-day cruise liner. The troop ship was 622 feet long with a 76 foot beam. Its passenger capacity was a little over 5,000 with a complement of over 400 sailors. On our Baltic cruise we were seated at a table with a former Marine who sailed on the Breckinridge at about the same time that I did. It took him over fifty years before he ventured on another ship, that's how bad the conditions were on that vessel.

We boarded launches for about a 15 minute ride to the troop transport. The rough bay water caused many of the men to become seasick or nauseous. I was assigned a modified bunk-type-hammock for the next two weeks that seemed to sway to the motion of the ship. To make matters worse, there was another hammock above mine, which also moved slightly to the rhythm of the ship and added to my uncomfortable feeling of nausea. To make matters even more intolerable, the dinner for the first evening was chili con carne, (military ingenuity), which didn't remain in our stomachs very long once we were underway. So the result was thousands of seasick men starting out on a two week voyage. A picture of the WWII- Korean-Vietnam War highly decorated ship USS General J.C. Breckinridge follows:

I was lucky to be on restricted sick-duty due to my appendix operation and didn't have to serve K.P. (kitchen patrol). Many of the men told me the horror stories of being below deck in temperatures of up to 100 degrees, cleaning pots, pans and mopping wet greasy floors. The July temperatures stayed with us for the whole trip, and combined with the rough seas kept many of the soldiers and sailors seasick.

As I was on special restricted sick-duty, I was able to spend a great deal of time, without supervision, at the ship's library where there was a comfortable reading chair that I made good use of. It was there that I read my first book from beginning to end. I didn't choose the novel Rebecca, by Daphne Du Maurier by choice; it was one of the few remaining books available on the shelves that looked easy to read. It was about 350 pages; the back cover attracted my attention stating that it was a crime, mystery and romance novel, just what I was looking for to pass the time of day, while I goofed off for two weeks. The opening line was "Last night I dreamt I went to Manderley again." The story was about a young girl's transition into womanhood while working as a companion to a rich American woman vacationing on the French Riviera. She becomes involved with a wealthy Englishman and after a few weeks of courtship she marries her prince charming and retires to his mansion, Manderley. From that point on, murder, mystery and treachery come into play. . . .

I really got into the book which took about a week to finish. I searched the bookshelves for another exciting experience and found the translated version of "The Twelve Caesars," written by Gaius Suetonius Tranquillus in 121 AD, who was the personal secretary to Emperor Hadrian. He wrote about the lives of the first twelve Caesars in detail. I never thought I could become so engrossed in the written word. As a young lad I always resisted reading the Bible that my father insisted I read out-loud during our prayer sessions. I think it turned me off to reading in general, and it took me many years to overcome my aversion to literature. Being alone in the library on a ship heading for Japan, I finally began to overcome my distaste for reading and began to absorb and become intrigued by the history of the first twelve Caesars. Suetonius wrote about their lives:

Julius Caesar, (46-44 BCE), was the first Caesar (family name), he was murdered by fellow Romans.

Augustus-Octavius, (31 BCE-14 ACE), Caesar's nephew and adopted son, was poisoned by his wife.

Tiberius, (14-37 ACE), died of natural causes.

Caligula, (the hated one), (37-41 ACE), was murdered by fellow Romans.

Claudius, (41-54 ACE), was poisoned by his wife.

Nero, (the fiddler), (54-68 ACE), was forced to commit suicide.

Galba, (less than one year), was murdered by fellow Romans.

Otho, (less than one year), committed suicide.

Vitellius, (less than one year), was murdered by fellow Romans.

Vespasian, (69-79 ACE), died of natural causes.

Titus, (79-81), died of natural causes.

Domitian, (81-96), was murdered; he was the last of the Caesar family to rule the Roman Empire.

After reading about the history of the 140 turbulent years of the Roman Empire under the assortment of erratic Caesars, I was beginning to doubt the validity of its glorious existence. That is until I read about Emperor Trajan (98-117 ACE), who seemed to magically bring sanity to the throne and empire. He rebuilt Rome, stabilized the Senate and curtailed civil war, while expanding the empire's boundaries far beyond its previous borders. That book began my adventure and passion with reading about ancient history. While waiting for reassignment from Nagoya, Japan, I finally opened the pocket Bible that my father gave me for safekeeping. I began reading the Old Testament first and then continued with the New Testament. It took me a couple of years, on and off, to get through the two books, but I did it and loved every minute of it. For some unexplained reason, I never told my father about my voluntarily reading his favorite scriptures. My character-chain was growing as I learned that: "No plans are written in stone," "When working for a large organization, don't anticipate future actions, just go with the flow," and "The older I got, the smarter my father became."

Our first stop was Pusan Harbor, South Korea to deliver supplies and troops to reinforce our fighting forces. It took a couple of days to unload the supplies and the approximately 5,000 soldiers. Watching the endless lines of men disembarking was a depressing scene that I still carry with me today. I wondered which of my young comrades would join the ranks of the already 35,000-plus dead and 198,000 wounded in Korea.

Luckily an armistice was signed at the end of the month on July 27, 1953. Although the document was signed, it took many months for the North Koreans to stop fighting and to abide, somewhat, to the terms of the agreement. Hundreds of weary soldiers boarded the ship for R&R (Rest and Rehabilitation) in Tokyo, Japan. We arrived in Tokyo Harbor, carefully docked at the huge pier and unloaded the happy soldiers, including me, at the humongous port where a military information center was set up for our convenience. I was informed that I would be taking an overnight train from Tokyo to Nagoya, (approximately 200 miles), that evening. It was good to get my land-legs back and feel steady again on solid ground. The big surprise was that I was assigned to a sleeping car with a soft private bunk bed, a big improvement from the accommodations on the Breckinridge.

Nagoya AFB was the headquarters of the 5th Air Force. I was excited that my assignment was going to be as a radio operator on a bomber. I stayed at the base for over a month, which gave me an opportunity to spend time in the large city of Nagoya that had a population at that time of about one million people. The city was heavily bombed during WWII by our B29s, their main target being the Mitsubishi Aircraft Engine Works. It's estimated that general firebombing destroyed over 100,000 buildings with over 500,000 people displaced. Considering that I was there only eight years after the end of the war, there wasn't a trace of any destruction to be seen throughout the large city. What was surprising was that the Japanese people were very cordial and polite to U.S. servicemen. While waiting for reassignment I had an opportunity to catch up for all the years of avoiding the written page and read as many books as I could get my hands on. I also had an opportunity to learn how to play tennis at the base's recreation center. I actually got pretty good at the game and wouldn't you know, just as I developed my stride, orders came for me to ship out; my new assignment was not on an Air Force bomber, but it was to relocate to an Army base outside of Tokyo for further assignment, hopefully my last.

Well, this time my transportation was more in keeping with being in a flying organization. I flew the whole 200 miles back to Tokyo in a C-47 twin-engine-prop troop transport. A picture of the plane follows:

The plane had the same seating arrangements as its bigger sister, the C-54. About 30 men sat side-by-side, but this time we had to wear our parachutes and the flight sergeant didn't have any prepared speeches to scare us with, probably because some of the passengers were officers. This time we were given explicit instructions on the proper use of parachutes in case of an emergency, and the proper protocol for jumping from the aircraft.

The Army base that I was assigned to was a god-forsaken swamp. The stench from raw sewage and the urine deposited by the local residents at will, made me gag and wish I were back on the Breckinridge breathing in the fresh salt Pacific Ocean air. I was assigned to a tent that was already occupied by nine other airmen, who were also waiting for reassignments. We slept on cots that required overhead mosquitoes-nets to protect us from the flying cannibals that seemed to be everywhere. After my first uncomfortable night sleeping on a cot that seemed to be made out of concrete, I awoke the next morning to the throbs and pain of my right arm that was bitten unmercifully. The blood-suckers used my right arm for their BBQ while it rested on the net. I was beginning to wonder if joining the military wasn't a mistake. I had been in the Air Force for less than a year, and had ended up in hospitals at Sampson AFB in New York for a trimming, Francis E. Warren AFB in Wyoming with pneumonia, and the Oakland Naval Base for an appendectomy. My first air flight resulted in a forced landing. My two week experience on the Breckinridge in sweltering heat and swelling seas had me seasick and nauseous for most of the trip. I was being shipped from one base to another with no final destination in sight, and the prospect of staying in a mosquito infested swamp for an undetermined period of time was really giving me doubts about my decision making abilities. Even though none of these events were of my choosing, it seemed that providence was toying with my patience and endurance.

Fortunately I only stayed in the hell-hole a couple of days before receiving my orders to relocate to the city of Tokyo. I was taken by jeep to the heart of Tokyo and dropped off at the 8-story New Kaijo Building, which was located across the street from the Imperial Palace. I stared at the building, frozen in disbelief that this was going to be my residence for the next three years. What a great turn of events, hopefully for the better. The large square lobby had a dining hall (not a mess hall), a PX (Post Exchange), barber shop and a reception desk. After producing my orders, I was directed to an elevator that took me to the eighth floor where my future home awaited me. It was a nice size room that I shared with two other airmen. A picture of the New Kaijo Building follows:

The New Kaijo Building is in the middle of the picture with the Airmen's Club across the street at the left, and the Imperial Palace's moat in the foreground.

We had regular single beds with thick mattresses, private standup lockers and a personal room boy. It was the United States' policy that servicemen had to use the locals as valets, probably to provide jobs for them and to get money into their local economy. Our room boy, Shunsuki, made our beds, took care of our laundry, shined our shoes and did other menial tasks for us, all for ten dollars a month from each occupant. After the horrible swamp experience, I thought that I had died and went to heaven, but the fun was just beginning.

My work assignment was on the same boulevard just two city streets away in the Meiji Building, another high rise structure facing the Imperial Palace. A photo of that building follows:

The Air Force's main communication center was located in the building; I was thrilled at becoming an integral part of that elaborate system. My character-chain was growing by leaps and bounds; I learned never to discount the importance of luck. "Plans are made while God smiles, but if He doesn't wink His approval, you're up the creek without a paddle." So I took it all in stride and went with the flow. My job was to transmit military code to Hawaii and other key bases throughout the Pacific. What I mean by code was typing scrambled words and numbers at high speed, a very tedious task, but once I got use to the routine, it became just another job. We also had to transmit facsimiles of weather map forecasts to Korea and Hawaii that were used in planning military operations, especially important for the Air Force and Naval Air Commands, in determining if it was safe for their planes to take-off and go into action.

I became friendly with our shift commander, Major Johnson. He coaxed me into drawing maps that we transmitted throughout the Pacific, which added another dimension to my job description, and allowed me to get my second stripe sooner than expected. He also insisted that I get my GED, (General Equivalency High School Diploma). His prompting and the fact that the men I worked with were high school graduates and knew so much more than I did scholastically, such as reading, writing and arithmetic, made me go head-over-heels into the studies that were required to complete the subjects needed to take the GED exams. The courses were given by the United States Armed Forces Institute (USAFI) which I attended religiously in Japan and back home at Mitchel AFB on Long Island; it took two years before I took the exams and finally received my diploma. A copy of my certificates follows:

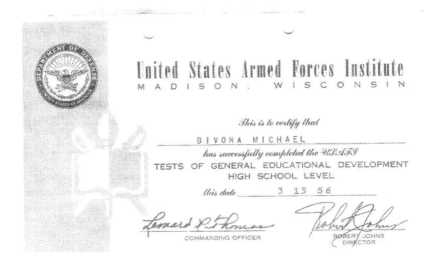

Living in a cosmopolitan city like Tokyo was quite different from the places that I grew up. Although I was born and bred in Brooklyn, which is a large borough with a population in the millions, my experience was mostly a neighborhood one, consisting of family and mostly Italian-American friends. Tokyo was a whole different place, a mirror of Manhattan, New York, which I visited briefly on special occasions, like seeing the latest movies on the new large Cinemascope screens, and working at part time jobs for short periods of time. Now I was in a metropolis that would be my home for the next three years, and I was feeling pretty good about it; I felt that I had arrived and was at a place that I belonged. A nice touch to my new experience was our dining hall. On other military installations the procedure was to wait on line with tray in hand and have food plopped onto our silver compartmentalized trays. Not so at the New Kaijo; we had menus, waiters from the local population took our orders as if we were in a restaurant, and politely served us while smiling throughout the event. I knew that it would be very easy to get used to my new lifestyle. The only downside to the job was that I had to work two week shifts. Two weeks during the daytime from 8 AM to 4 PM, in the evenings from 4 PM to 12 AM, and the morning shift from 12 AM to 8 AM. After each two week shift, in addition to getting two regular days off during the week, I got an additional three days off to get my body's time clock adjusted back to normal, if that was possible. Just when I thought I was back on track, the system would start all over again, to a point that I would lose sight of what day of the week it was.

Across from the New Kaijo on the side street was the Airmen's Club. There were three sections; officers, noncoms (noncommissioned officers-sergeants) and enlisted men (below rank of sergeant). We all shared the same entrance that was lined with slot machines and ornate mirrored walls. I dropped many a coin into the slots, but don't remember ever winning one cent. Each of the venues had its own dining room and nightclub. After payday my buddies and I made a point of dining at the plush enlisted men's restaurant. We would all order filet mignon steaks, smothered with bacon and the largest baked potato in existence, complemented with endless glasses of Nippon Beer. For most of us it was the first time that we were ever served in such an upscale eatery and the first time that we ever tasted such an amazing delicious piece of meat. The nightclub was also a first for many of us. Most of us had never been at a hall where a big seventeen piece band played music. In addition, the waiters treated us as if we were VIPs. We were allowed to bring girls into the club to spend the evening eating, drinking and dancing, at very reasonable prices. At that time the exchange rate was 360 yen to the dollar; similar entertainment at the local clubs was very expensive for enlisted men, so we spent many an evening enjoying the facilities that our government provided for us at reasonable prices; that is if you could get past the slot machines. The building also had a state-of-the-art gym with a boxing ring. It was mandatory that we spend several hours a week at the gym keeping in shape just in case we needed our muscles for military purposes.

At the end of my first month in Japan, an armistice was signed with North Korea. The city had a celebration that included fireworks displays by the Japanese and U.S. military, and lots of hoorays and hugs between the soldiers and civilians. At the tender age of nineteen, I experienced the thrill of a war coming to an end and the resultant relief that came with it from the anxiety of possibly being shipped to the war zone in Korea, where our boys died by the tens-of-thousands. It took a few months before the fighting actually stopped. In the meantime the military was starting to make arrangements to ship soldiers back to the states. For the next couple of years, our fighting troops would pass through Tokyo on R&R leave before returning to their homes in the United States for discharge. But, as the treaty was tenuous, a large number of our troops remained in Korea and a substantial number in Japan as backup support in case of another military surprise from the North Koreans or the Chinese.

For the next couple of years, I kept busy studying for my GED tests and traveling around Japan when I had the opportunity, visiting many religious shrines and small towns. When traveling for pleasure we were not allowed to wear our uniforms, only civilian clothing. So I had to buy a nonmilitary wardrobe. Fortunately the prices at the PX were reasonable, so a couple of pairs of pants, some shirts and a jacket were sufficient. Being stationed in the heart of Tokyo put me close to movie theaters, restaurants, shopping and the famous Ginza Market; all of these were walking distance from the New Kaijo. The most popular entertainment venue in Tokyo was the Ernie Pyle Theater, named in honor of the famous American war correspondent who was killed in the Pacific during WWII. The theater was originally called Takarazuko Gekijo but was rechristened the Ernie Pyle Theater to pay tribute to the fallen battlefield journalist who wrote from a foot-soldier's point-of-view, and had a great following in the military and back home in the United States. It was a 2,000-plus seat theater that the GIs would fill to the rafters to see free shows by beloved entertainers such as Bob Hope, Louie Armstrong and Bing Crosby. It was also the main movie theater for Americans and Japanese, where all of the latest movies could be seen at very reasonable prices.

One of my favorite pastimes was shopping at the outdoor Ginza Market on Sundays with my special friend Meiko. A picture of her is below modeling with two of her friends; she is the beautiful girl on the right:

To mike love
miko.

It's difficult to describe the place; there were hundreds of street-vendors selling everything from rubberbands to household furniture. Restaurants, nightclubs and bars lined every street. Music and exotic food aromas also filled the air, tempting passersby to enter their establishments for food, drinks and other delights. There were also many department stores selling famous and not so famous designer clothing. The largest and most popular was the Mitsukoshi Department Store which was known as "The Harrods of Tokyo," housing such upscale shops as Tiffany & Co and Barney's Fifth Avenue. It was at the street-peddlers market that I learned the art of bargaining with pushcart peddlers, (isn't everyone a peddler?). I would put that talent to good use in the future, when dealing with business peddlers. Meiko would see something she was interested in buying, like a lamp, and ask the price. The peddler would state "Very cheap, ten dollars," she would say: "You're crazy, I'll give you two dollars," he would reply "You're crazy, best price eight dollars." After all the jostling back and forth she would give her final offer of five dollars, which he would accept while cursing. Of course, all of this went on in Japanese, but it wasn't difficult to get the drift of what was going on and after some practice I also became an expert hondler. Even though I perfected the art, when I walked away from the cursing peddlers with my prize, I always got the feeling that I didn't get such a bargain.

When I was stationed in Tokyo a little over a year, I was asked if I would like to work in the Imperial Palace as a liaison between the Japanese meteorologists and their counterparts in the Air Force. I jumped at the opportunity to work with the locals and begin my day at 8 AM until 4 PM, instead of the exhausting rotating shifts that kept me in a state of confusion. The assignment also added my third stripe, I became a sergeant and was able to eat in the noncommissioned officers' dining hall which entitled me to a lower bow from the Japanese staff at the New Kaijo, (the lower the bow, the more honorable the person). Every morning I was picked up by jeep and driven to the communication station on the palace grounds, which made my head swell and gave me an exhilarating feeling of importance. My character-chain was still expanding; I realized that my father was sometimes right, that "Hard work, following instructions and producing quality results, opens many doors of opportunity." Another saying of his that kept popping into my mind as I made difficult decisions was, "The easiest person for you to fool is yourself." During my early years I became very proficient at fooling myself; it seemed that when I acted impulsively, I always had lots of time to regret my quick decisions.

The 284-acres Imperial Palace complex was the heart of Tokyo and of Japan. The Imperial Family resided in their temporary quarters on the palace grounds as their original residence was destroyed by allied bombing during WWII and wasn't restored to its splendor until 1968 long after I left Japan. The Japanese take their monarchs very seriously and live their lives to a great extent by the preaching and dictates of the emperor. The fact that I was working in the Imperial Palace complex made me a very honored and special person to the Japanese people that I came into contact with. The palace grounds are surrounded by a moat, a gray-stone-wall, with beautiful stoned bridges running across the moat, and oriental spire rooftops that gave the appearance of a heavenly place, especially since the grounds are slightly elevated from the street level. Passing over the bridges you can't help noticing the abundance of royal white swans guarding the palace and hissing and trumpeting their presence while reminding everyone that they are entering hallowed grounds and to act accordingly. Entering the gated stronghold over the Nijubashi Bridge, which means double bridge due to its reflection in the water that makes it look like there is also a mirrored bridge below, led to the interior of the walled stronghold. Entering in early spring when cherry blossoms were in bloom and the surrounding gardens were showing off their treasures, gave me the feeling that I was entering a beautiful floral painting; the colors were breathtaking and the fragrance soothing to the soul. The splendor of the four royal gardens within the palace walls are a testament to the passion that the Japanese people have for floral beauty. The Outer Garden is open to the public and is an inviting resting place for visitors to bring their lunch and enjoy the surrounding beauty of the landscape. The Fukiage Garden is where the Imperial Palace royal residents and the offices of the Imperial Household Agency were located. The East Garden is the home to many training centers for traditional crafts and occupations, and the Kitanomaru National Garden has various museums to share its floral beauty. These gardens are separated by moats, walls and very large boulders. I enjoyed having lunch at the Outer Garden but especially liked walking through the East Garden, which was also open to the public. It boasted a dense forest and a collection of trees with at least one representative from each of Japan's 47 prefectures. This garden was designed as a place for quiet meditation and rejuvenation. It featured well-tended paths lined with azaleas, zigzag bridges to confuse evil spirits, as they can only walk in straight lines, and ponds full of koi fish. Among the buildings in the East Garden are Archery Hall, Kendo and Judo Hall, the Music Department, the Imperial Stables and the Imperial Guard House. Special attractions to me were an extraordinary 350-year-old "Bonsai Tree" in the Garden behind the imperial residence and a 400-year-old "Crab Tree" and 500-year old "Juniper Tree," which I was able to see on one of the two days a year that the restricted palace grounds were open to the public. On January 2nd and on his birthday, December 23rd, the Emperor made public appearances; I was fortunate to see Emperor Hirohito when he presented himself several times during his January appearance.

Well, the big question, what was the Air Force doing in the palace? Since the grounds of the palace were more stable than the surrounding areas and buffered by a moat that surrounded the premises, it was one of the few places in Tokyo where seismographic equipment that measured the earth's tremors could be installed without picking up the vibrations from the outside automobile traffic and the heavy building equipment that was at work all over the city. The seismographic equipment was the property of the United States and required a representative to be present to make sure that it was being used in accordance with the rules laid down by the occupying military forces. There were about twenty Japanese locals working at the station. One of my benefits was that about once a month one of them would invite me to their home for dinner and to meet their family and friends. A culture shock was that the women would serve the men their meals while they ate in separate rooms. After the meal the women would join us for tea and social discussions, and a question and answer session. They invariably had lists of written questions about the United States that they would ask, and then would meticulously record the answers next to the questions on their lists. A question that came up often and seemed to puzzle them was: "How could the country that defeated the Japanese Empire be losing the war against the inferior Koreans?" A good question of which I had no valid answer so I would respond, "I don't know." My character-chain grew immensely from these hospitable dinners, many of the things Americans take for granted, like eating and enjoying family and friends in mixed company are not widely practiced in Japan. I wondered how my two spirited sisters would react to such subordinate treatment. Another benefit was eating lots of delicious homemade Japanese food, which fifty years later is still one of my favorite delights. Since I spent so much time with the locals, I did manage to pick up some of the language pretty well, but their writing was a puzzlement to me. I didn't have much time to study the intricate pictured language as my stay in Tokyo would soon be cut short by one year. A picture of the Imperial Palace, the protective moat and the Nijubashi Bridge (double bridge) is below:

A picture of me standing in front one of a smaller building of the Palace follows:

The weather in Tokyo was similar to New York City, so it didn't take too long to adjust and feel comfortable with the temperature changes, except that it could get excessively hot in the summer due to the ten-million-plus people that resided in the area, and the great number of cars that threw off an enormous amount of heat and carbon monoxide fumes from their engines. My favorite method of transportation was the metro-train-system. It has an astonishing procedure for handling the incredible amount of passengers that rely on it to commute. Everyone waits on the station platform in designated lines. The platforms are marked where the train doors will stop and open. When the doors open the orderly platform dwellers file single line into the train, when the cars are filled, then the remaining passengers on the platform push the people in front of them into the cars, politely, until there isn't an inch of unoccupied space left. When the lines are long, there are platform attendants wearing white gloves that gently shove the riders into the cars. Well, that was when I was there in 1953-55 when the population was ten-million, currently the population has doubled, I can just imagine the organized chaos that takes place when taking the metro today.

In 1955 the Korean War was basically over and the need for our presence in Japan in great numbers was no longer necessary. So we were given a choice of remaining for our original three year tour-of-duty or of going home after two years. My job at the palace after a year was getting quite boring. I missed the camaraderie of my fellow airmen, I was getting the feeling I was outside the group that I had become so friendly with. Also, my family wrote many letters telling me how much they all enjoyed living in the same neighborhood, far from the hectic streets of Liberty and Pitkin Avenues. My father and brother Vic bought a two-family house on Montauk Avenue in a residential section of East New York. My sister Anne rented an apartment on the same street about a hundred yards away. If I returned home, for the first time in my life I would be living on a quiet street with my whole family on one block. My father wrote and told me that when I returned there would be a bedroom that I wouldn't have to share with anyone; previously I slept with my brother Vic or my father. So considering all the alternatives, I decided to return home to the U.S. after staying two years in Japan, the big question was, home to where? There was an opening for my job description at Mitchel Field in Garden City, Long Island, and one at Sampson AFB in upstate New York. So wanting the Long Island assignment I put in as first choice the one at Sampson AFB, hoping that the military's sense of reasoning would result in my getting the second choice. Within one month I received orders that I was being assigned to Mitchel Field, just as I predicted, luckily the base was just 25 minutes from our new home on Montauk Avenue. Before leaving I was offered an opportunity to stay in Japan until I was discharged, which was a little over one year. A Japanese electronics company was recruiting Americans for their communication and organizational skills. They were paying sign-up bonuses of $2,000, which was a lot of money in those days, to stay on and work for them in the electronics field, (my yearly salary was $2,400). It was tempting, but my grandmother's meatballs and spaghetti were calling me, and a private room in our new home was too much to resist, so I turned down the offer. Many of my buddies found the offer too tempting to pass up, especially for those who married Japanese girls.

Saying goodbye to my buddies and the Japanese personnel I worked with was difficult to say the least. I was given a going away party by the airmen in my group, which was also attended by the officers in our communication center. It was at the Airmen's Club across the street from our billet. About twenty-five of my friends chipped in and gave me an unforgettable going away bash that lasted till the club closed at 1AM. A seventeen piece "Glen Miller" copy-band provided music throughout the evening, while we drank and danced with our local girlfriends until we were filled to capacity, both physically and mentally. I was lucky to have a second going away party by my Japanese coworkers at the Imperial Palace. The event was more subdued, but we did have a couple of hours of good sushi, lots of sake', and lots of farewell hugs. A picture of three of my closest friends, Jonsan, Fredsan and Ricksan follows. It seems from the picture that I was beginning to look like my fellow workers, who by the way called me Mikesan:

I relocated to Yokohama AFB to await my transportation back to the United States. After hanging around for a couple of weeks I received my orders to ship, not fly, back to the U.S. on the old faithful troop carrier USS General J.C. Breckinridge. It still was an ugly dark gray and was no better or worse from wear and tear. The trip back to the States was a lot smoother than my first voyage to Japan, no chili con carnie was served, and the seas were in our favor, so whatever seasickness there was on board was minor. We stopped at Korea to pick up troops and supplies, then on to Formosa (Taiwan) and then to Hawaii. We were not allowed to leave the ship to relax and explore the beautiful islands because each stop was only for a day. We arrived at Oakland, California after cruising on the calm Pacific Ocean for over two weeks, I stumbled off of the ship and around the docks until I got my land-legs back. At that point I was on my own for a 30 day furlough, plus 5 days traveling time. When I first landed in California, which was more than two years ago, I was a greenhorn airman, when I visited the second time I was 21, a sergeant and master of my domain. My main concern was how to travel home. Should I repeat the boring-tedious-endless train ride in the opposite direction to New York or should I fly 3,000 miles across the country in a four-engine-prop-plane? (Jets were not used commercially at that time). The first time I flew in one of those planes from Sampson AFB in upstate New York to Francis E. Warren AFB in Cheyenne, Wyoming we had a forced landing in Nebraska which resulted in a hearing loss to my right ear. The rapid descent in the unpressurized plane caused me to lose most of my hearing in my right ear which resulted in a constant ringing in that ear. Weighing the circumstances and the fact that my return flight was in the hot month of July and the Boeing B-377 Stratocruiser that would transport me home was the state-of- the-art flying machine in 1955, with air conditioning, I decided to take the quicker more expensive ride home. The humongous plane was 110 feet long with a 141 foot wing span, with a cruising speed of 300 mph. It carried about 80 passengers in plush reclining seats, and the spacious cabin was decorated in bright welcoming colors. Its extra large cabin led to gold-colored dressing rooms and a circular staircase led to a lower-deck drinking lounge where attendants prepared hot meals upon request. The plane was like a flying luxury resort suite with all the conveniences, including air-conditioning, and hot and cold running water in the rest rooms. The flight to New York took over ten hours; the amenities on board were put to good use and made the long flight tolerable. Flying at 25,000 feet made many of the passengers nervous, including me. If it weren't for the spaciousness of the cabin and the other comforts, the flight home would have been a very frightening experience. The long journey gave me lots of time to read and think about my future. I still had over a year remaining of my four year enlistment and was seriously weighing my options of what my life would be after my discharge from the military. I realized that I didn't have too many; I could reenlist, continue my education, or try to find a good paying job in the communication field. A picture of the four-engine flying luxury hotel is below:

BOEING B.377. „Super Stratocruiser"   P.A.A.

It was amusing that at age 21, I was the first one in my family to own a car, (actually three cars), I was the first to fly on an airplane, (actually three planes), and probably the first to ride a horse, (many, many, horses). I was wondering if there were going to be any other firsts for me. Oh I almost forgot, I was also the first to get circumcised.

The B-377 bounced along the LaGuardia Airport runway and then came to a smooth stop, I'm sure that the passengers' prayers had something to do with our successful landing. My brother Vic was waiting for me at the airport, after hugging and kissing for about two minutes, we got in his black shiny Cadillac and drove to my new home at 360 Montauk Avenue. My whole family was waiting for me; my father Luciano Joseph, Grandma Tootsie Angelina, my sister, beautiful Anne Ambrico and her husband Lou and their three handsome kids, Dennis, Louis and RoseMargaret; my other beautiful sister Rosaria (Mae), and my gorgeous sister-in-law Rose and her two beautiful children, Joseph and Margaret. I was thrilled at the house that my father and brother purchased in a neighborhood that had mostly residential two-family houses. We hugged and kissed for the better part of the late afternoon, after the emotional exchange of affections, we all sat down for dinner in the semi-finished basement which had an extended table that accommodated all of us. My grandmother's meatballs, sausages, chicken, veal and spaghetti were a meal from heaven. We spent all evening eating, kissing and reminiscing about old times. My picture in dress-uniform at that time follows:

After a couple of days, I gave out the presents that returned with me from Japan. The boys got silk black jackets with embroidered dragons on the backs. The girls received Japanese dolls dressed in beautifully stitched kimonos. My father and brother received cuff links and a tie pin with oriental designs. My grandmother received a silk scarf. My sisters received pearl 24 karate gold rings and Rose received a pendulum clock in a glass case. My brother-in-law Lou received a silver keychain with a gold Air Force emblem. I spent the first days just hanging around the house enjoying the company of my grandmother, Angelina, and my sisters Anne, Mae and Rose. It didn't take too long for me to get restless. My priority was to buy a car as soon as possible so I could travel the 25 miles to Mitchel AFB at will instead of taking the Long Island Railroad. I found a beautiful two-door 1950 Chevrolet Sport Coupe in perfect condition that one of our neighbors was selling. It was dark blue and had a like-new-shine. I paid $300 for my fourth car and immediately returned to my old neighborhood on Pitkin Avenue to visit my childhood buddies. A picture of a twin Chevy follows:

I drove to Pitkin and Van Siclen Avenues hoping to find some of my buddies there. Well it didn't take too long to locate the human-street-fixtures. My friends were still hanging around the street corners as if frozen in time. I stopped briefly to catch up with them and to see if anything new had happened in their lives. Nothing new happened; they were still doing the same old things and talking about the same old nonsense. I drove to my friend Paul Maggio's house and luckily caught him in. He told me that his dad had passed away when he was stationed overseas and had to come home for the funeral. His father was a special person; he always gave us a knowing wink when he caught us doing something questionable. We did lots of catching up about where we were stationed in the Air Force. He told me that he was interested in becoming a male nurse, but was concerned about the cost and the amount of time it would take to complete the required courses. Eventually he not only succeeded, but ended up owning a nursing home in Patchogue, N.Y. After that meeting we wouldn't be in contact with each other for over 20-years, but providence was instrumental in our meeting through mutual friends, and we would not only resume our friendship, but we would have many successful business dealings together.

My thirty days furlough passed quickly, I ate incredible food with my wonderful family, slept late as often as I could, made new friends on the block and then packed my bags and headed on my 25-mile trip to Mitchel AFB. I reported for duty, the first order of the day was my living accommodations. I was assigned to a room that I shared with one other airman in a pretty modern building that had ample space for clothing and a desk; a big improvement from my previous sleeping arrangements in the United States. It had a regular single bed and built-in closets, not a bad place to end my military career. My new job assignment was in the code section that was integrated with a new telecommunication system which included modern day computers that were so big that they took up half of our work area. I shared the center with six other soldiers; it didn't take long for me to get comfortable and friendly with my fellow airmen. After a couple of months at the base, I qualified to live off-base with a generous allowance, so I moved my gear back to Montauk Avenue and for the next year traveled to Mitchel Field every workday. It was the same as being a civilian, steady hours, a steady paycheck, plus a nice living allowance, which I gave to my father for my upkeep. During that time two major events happened, I passed the GED exams, which made me the second one in my immediate family with a high school diploma, (my mother Margaret was the first), and my beloved grandmother Angelina (Tootsie) Bivona Messina passed away. She was called Grandma Tootsie by her grandchildren and great grandchildren to distinguish her from the other grandmothers in their families. Her name came from the frankfurter dog (Dachshund) named Tootsie that I gave her as a birthday present when I was about 16-years old to replace her recently deceased police dog, whom she loved dearly.

The year passed quickly and before I knew it I was faced with the decision of remaining in the Air Force or becoming a civilian. I was offered three incentives to remain in the military; a $2,500 reenlistment bonus, my fourth stripe, and a guarantee that I would remain at Mitchel Field for at least two years. The bonus was almost a year's salary and surpassed my four-years of savings by $1,000. The extra stripe meant a large increase in salary, the only downside was that I would have to move back to the base and become one of the communication center's supervisors. At the same time I was offered a job with RCA Communications in Manhattan. It was the end of 1956 and I must say I was nervous, so I discussed my situation with my father and brother Vic, they both thought leaving the military was the best choice and certainly would offer greater opportunities for my future. After many grueling weeks in which I must have changed my mind a hundred times, I decided that leaving the Air Force and starting over again to face new challenges was my best decision. At the age of 22 my mature character chose the unknown with its inherent risks and possible rewards, to the more familiar life in the military. That was the beginning of my taking many journeys into the unknown which I hoped would result in positive outcomes.

RCA Communications was the largest teletype company in the world at that time. I loved being a part of an international organization, what I didn't like was working shifts. I was back to the dizzying work schedule that resulted in my losing track of time and creating lots of stress in my single social lifestyle. I remember going to work in Manhattan on a Saturday and was shocked to find it was my day off. So when the opportunity came for me to fill a position at General Tire and Rubber Corp.'s Headquarters in Manhattan, I jumped at the chance. It was a whole new experience; I had to set up teletype systems in their New York office and multiple New Jersey warehouses. After the systems were in place and fully operational, we would gradually replace that outdated mode of communicating with the new kid on the block, "Univac Computers."

It seemed that I found the perfect job. I was making a good salary, I was involved with the latest communication technology, computers, and I had no supervisors. It seemed that every time I got comfortable with a job, a radical change took place. The change took place when I was at the Palladium Dance Hall in Manhattan which was a great singles' hang-out at that time. Providence was responsible for my bumping into an old friend, Arnie. He joined the Navy about a year before I went into the military and told me he was attending classes at New York University (NYU), majoring in physical education. I asked how he got into college being that he didn't graduate high school. He said it was easy, he received his GED while in the Navy and passed the entrance exams at NYU, everything else was history. His story intrigued me. While growing up he was not considered the sharpest pencil in the box, and I knew I had as much on the ball as he did, so I wondered if I could also get into college? I immediately contacted the Veterans Administration and filled out all the required forms. Prerequisites for processing the documents were that my GED scores meet above average standards, which they did, and I would also have to take an aptitude test (IQ test) to see what I was qualified to study in college. So in September 1957, eleven months after I was discharged from the Air Force, I was a freshman at Long Island University. I never intended to spend more than a year there; my objective was to have college attendance on my resume so I could apply for better paying jobs. At the rate I was going, I figured that my lifetime earnings would be around $300,000, which was at about the same earnings as my father, which didn't make me too happy.

I got by the first semester which required passing two remedial no credit courses in English and Algebra. I passed those courses with A's and received Bs and a C in my other classes. During the second semester I was able to take 18 credits and received all Bs and an A in English. What a surprise it was for me to have passed all the courses and all it took was endless studying, lots of sweating and a determination to succeed. The rest is history, I continued with my university experience, and by attending accelerated classes during the summer months, I was able to graduate in a little over three years. So in June 1960, I was a college graduate with a Bachelor of Science Degree, with an accounting major and an economic minor. At that point, my character was pretty much in place, and I was pretty much the person that I would be for the rest of my life. I was 26 years old with a college degree that I was sure would open many doors of opportunity for me in the job market and in life. I was also the first one in my family to graduate college, much to the delight of my father, who was convinced that his prayers got me through the rough spots, which I have no doubt was true. The only problem I had was that I was broke. I spent all of my military savings to sustain myself. The small salaries I earned working in the university's Accounting Department and for the accounting professors in their private practices only amounted to pocket-money. I had a new job paying $80.00 a week, which didn't help me get a loan at Citibank because I hadn't started working yet. I needed a couple of suits, shirts, shoes, socks and ties to start my new job, and no money to buy them with. The total cost of the items was about $300.00. No one in my family had money to loan me as they all lived from paycheck to paycheck, but with my brother Vic as a co-signer I was able to borrow the money from Citibank at three-percent interest. I went shopping for the first time in my life with lots of money in my pockets and purchased enough clothing to make me look like a bona fide accountant. I had over $100 left after my spending spree, so I hunted for a car that was an integral part of my traveling job, and of course, a major part of my single social life. A neighbor was selling a 1952 Dodge 4 door Sedan. The engine was in perfect condition but the body paint was discolored and rusted. So for $125 dollars I purchased my fifth car, my father gave me the extra $25 so

I could make the purchase. It took me months to sand the rust spots and smooth out the many rough surfaces. With the help of my brother Vic, the car was ready for a $29.95 paint job. After the painting and baking process the car had a new face covering an old body. The emerald green color was outstanding and caused everyone to stare at the vehicle when I passed by. A picture of a similar wreck follows:

My first accounting job was with the prestigious accounting firm of David B. Jacobs, Certified Public Accountants, at 9 Rector Street in Manhattan; I had a new wardrobe; I had a car that looked shiny new and I had lots of confidence in what the future had in store for me. At age 26 most of my character-links were in place and I was ready to face whatever fate would throw my way.

Chapter Two - Turning Points in my Life

Life is a series of turning points that become chain reactions, one turn leading into another. Some are major events that dramatically alter the course of our lives; others are often small insignificant turns that guide us to another direction. Turning points can be involuntary and caused by others, such as parents moving to a new neighborhood, or school choices made by parents for their children, or in my family's case, a parent deciding to change religions. These are turns in our lives that are caused by other people's decisions that profoundly impact our futures. Other involuntary turning points are dictated by providence, such as death, sickness, natural disasters, accidents or as we all have experienced, a drastic drop in the stock market; all of which can and have changed the direction of our lives, whether we were an actual party to the event or are affected by its ripple effect. My use of the word providence is intentional; I could have used any of its synonyms, such as: outside influence, external circumstances, fate, chance, luck or destiny, but I chose providence because the word sounds more neutral than the alternatives; it has less of a religious connotation. If religious beliefs are responsible for all of our actions and turning points are preordained, then everything that happens in our lives is out of our control and is the will of God. I do not believe this to be true and will not approach my story from that point of view.

Voluntary turning points result from decisions that we make when we have options; we consider all of the available facts and hopefully chose the one that is best for us. Within the voluntary decision making process there are also those that are made without forethought or in the heat of the moment when one is angry, or in a passionate situation. Needless to say, we have all experienced many of the above causes that have affected our lives, and have reflected often on the impact they have had on us and to those in our sphere of influence. We have all looked back, at one time or another, and asked ourselves where we would be today if certain decisions or events had been different. Some common considerations are: where would I be today if I went to college? Where would I be today if I married someone else? Where would I be today if I had no kids? Where would I be today if I bought Hathaway-Berkshire at $10.00 a share? It's now selling for over $80,000.00 per share. Where would I be today if my parents didn't divorce or if they hadn't died prematurely? When considering the above turns that apply to me, I can more clearly answer my children's and friends' question: "How did you go from not attending high school to becoming a Certified Public Accountant with his own accounting firm; the treasurer and part owner of a publicly traded computer company; a magazine writer; a book author; a passionate boating enthusiast; an avid history book collector; a dancing aficionado and the recipient of the '2007 Distinguished Alumni Achievement Award' from Long Island University?"

My first turning point was involuntary, it happened when I was in my mother Margaret's uterus. It had to do with my father, Luciano Joseph Bivona, who was from a long line of Catholics, and who, during the Great Depression (1929-1939) decided that changing religions would bring him some relief from the financial crisis that he and his family were experiencing. So when I was born, my father's decision to change religions, made me at birth, a Seventh Day Adventist instead of a Catholic. My brother Victor and sisters Anne and Mae took the brunt of his radical decision, as they were raised in the Catholic faith and had to make changes in their way of thinking and worshiping. The Catholic Church, according to the doctrine of my father's new religion, had become their enemy and the reason for many of the things that were wrong in the world. His voluntary change of direction would haunt and cause a considerable amount of conflict, guilt and mental anguish in the lives of my sisters till their dying days. The impact on my life was not so profound, as I was born into the religion and went along with the flow. But his decision to adhere to the strict discipline and worshiping practices of his new faith did become a major factor in many of the decisions I made during my life, that resulted in major turning points, some leading to beneficial and productive paths, and others to roads that were rough and sometimes dangerous.

Another event that helped mold the way I thought and guided me through the many turning points in my life happened when I was about ten years old. It was during WWII, my father had a steady good paying job for the first time in many years, so he saved enough money to reclaim my mother's hocked engagement ring. We lived on Cleveland Street at that time, so it was an easy walk to Gilibertes' Pharmacy on Cleveland Street and Liberty Avenue, right across from my birth place. My father told me that he borrowed money and put my mother's diamond engagement ring up for collateral during the hard financial times of the Depression. He was going to pay the loan back plus three years interest and then surprise my mother with the ring as an anniversary present. His pockets were bulging with the $300.00 that he saved to pay off his debt. My mother worked for the Gilibertes who lived across the street from us. She took care of the store owner's elderly mother to earn money to help support the family during those difficult financial times. My father told me that things got so bad financially that he had to join the many other unemployed people on the government handout bread lines to bring food home so we could survive; the program was called "Home Relief." The only money he could scrape together at that time was from repairing sewing machines and from part time work in the garment industry. He was beaming with pride to be in a position to repay his loan and retrieve my mother's diamond engagement ring. We entered the pharmacy and went directly to the owner, they shook hands and my father said, "I'm here to pay my loan plus interests and get back my wife's ring." The pharmacist said: "Joe, I haven't seen or heard from you in over a year. I needed the money so I sold the ring." My father turned pale and then his face reddened, I thought he was going to punch the man in the face, but he very meekly shrugged his shoulders, took my hand and slowly dragged himself, with me in tow, out of the store. I don't think I knew what being embarrassed and humiliated was until that time. Tears were running down my father's face and it didn't take long before I followed with my own cascade. That moment didn't result in a major turning point in my life, but it did impress on me how valuable and important money was. Having it caused people to smile and be happy and the lack of it caused undue heartache and unhappiness. I realized that my father not having a steady job resulted in no cash in his pocket to buy the necessities to sustain his family, and created conditions where he had to sell his possessions to feed us. I promised that I would never be in the same position, so I always made sure I had a job, regardless of how menial it was, and I very rarely borrowed money. There was also the realization that being a store owner was a more desirable vocation than that of a worker whose financial success was dependent on someone else. Fortunately I was never witness to a depression of the magnitude that my father was trapped in, where 25% of the workforce in the United States were without jobs, with little help from the government. That experience lived with me for the rest of my life, and although it wasn't a turning point, it did dictate what roads I would take in the future when faced with choices that would result in turns in my life.

At the age of 13, providence dictated the most significant turning point in my life; the death of my beloved mother Margaret. She was only 47 years old when she passed on. Since my birth, she had trouble with heavy bleeding from fibroids, which she didn't get medical care for until it became life-threatening. She seemed to be sick more often than not from the heavy bleeding and finally consented to have a hysterectomy at probably one of the worst public hospitals in New York, if not the United States. The procedure, which today is a common and a pretty safe event, killed my mother. The operation was a success, according to the doctors at Unity Hospital, but the patient didn't survive. She ended up with septicemia (blood poisoning) and died a couple of days after the botched operation.

At the age of 13 I didn't quite understand what had happened, but I knew that she was sick because of my birth, and that I was somehow responsible for her death. Now that I look back on the tragic event, I realize that my rebellious actions were probably related to her demise. After that, I refused to go to church with my father who claimed that my mother was in a better place; I became a chronic truant in school and began to spend all of my time at pool halls and on the streets of Brooklyn with unsavory characters. The direction of my life certainly changed; I became an unruly juvenile delinquent and had many run-ins with the local police. The only reason I didn't end up in juvenile detention halls or reform schools was that the policemen on our neighborhood beat were sympathetic to my circumstances, so instead of confinement at the 75th Police Precinct, the patrolmen would occasionally whack me with their nightsticks on my butt and then take me home and turn me over to my overwrought sister Anne, who was my designated guardian. Luckily, as time passed I settled down and didn't join many of my friends that ended up going to prison; thanks mainly to the understanding police officers who foot-patrolled our neighborhood, and my sister Anne's patience and caring ways. After awhile I returned to school for a short period of time and fell in love with the typing teacher. I spent as much time in her class practicing as she would allow admiring her charm and exquisite proportions. Eventually I decided I would rather work than attend classes, so instead of joining my friends in school and doing teenage activities like playing punchball, handball and socializing with young girls, I chose a turn in the road that would lead to hard work at minimum wages, doing menial tasks. Talk about making mistakes, my heading out on my own at such an early age was a humongous one, but the turn was made, and I was on my way to becoming an independent, high spirited young person, capable, at times, of making sound decisions.

My next turn was the result of a combination of involuntary and voluntary events. There was a new small pox vaccine that everyone was advised to take, the closest place for the vaccination was the 75th Police Precinct which was only a few blocks from where I lived on Pitkin Avenue. Officer Maloney saw me waiting on line for my turn at being punctured and told me to come see him after my injection. He introduced me to a few boys my own age who were playing basketball. I tried the game that day and many days after, but I just didn't enjoy it, which I bluntly told him. He didn't give up on me and decided to loan me a baseball glove and ball which I gladly took and used as if they were extensions of my arms. I absolutely loved the game and got to play often with the PAL team from my district. As a reward for winning first place our team was treated to a trip outside of my neighborhood to the St. George Hotel, where I saw firsthand what was available on the other side of my restricted world. We spent the day enjoying the swimming pool, showers, gym, air conditioning and the camaraderie of each other; after all we were champions and made everyone we met know it. All that was required to step over the line into the world of comfort and luxury was money. I realized that no matter how hard I worked at the menial jobs that I was qualified for, I would rarely be able to afford the comforts that I so enjoyed that day, unless something in my life changed drastically. The two events, of being a champion and visiting the St. George Hotel, opened my eyes to the fact that I was trapped in my environment. I was bound first by my father's strict religious dictates that invariably restricted a person's ability to acquire and retain wealth, and secondly by a neighborhood where people's main objectives were to find jobs and bring money home to the family, quite often sacrificing their educations and any prospects for future development. Those events were pushing me, but I didn't know in what direction until providence played an unexpected card.

My wonderful step-grandfather Peter Messina died in the waiting room of the same hospital as my mother, after waiting for over two hours, of a chest aneurysm. He was an integral part of our lives as we spent all the major holidays and almost every Sunday at his home enjoying his delicious meals. He did most of the cooking and was assisted and directed by Grandma Tootsie, much to his playful annoyance. Our dinners were happy events, very different from my home where each meal was preceded by an elongated prayer, spiritual lectures and silence while eating. So visiting his home was always something we looked forward to. He had a red and green parrot that we would speak to and spend most of the day trying to get it to talk. His name was Pepe, unfortunately he only had a vocabulary of about four words, and no matter what tricks we tried to pull on him to get him to talk, all he could say was "hello, goodbye, come in and Pete." In addition to my grandfather's delicious Italian feasts, my grandmother always had toys and games for us to play, which was also missing in my home, as they were thought to be a frivolous waste of time and hard earned money. We always enjoyed playing games with our cousins who celebrated many of the holidays at my grandmother's table. They were the children of my deceased grandfather Victor's (my father's father), brother Joseph and were always welcomed at Tootsie's house.

Grandpa Pete's freshly cut six-foot-plus Xmas trees, and handmade ornaments, which he handcrafted into religious scenes, still returns to my memory when I decorate my tree every year. My passion for decorating and displaying my Xmas tree and my worldwide ornament collection is driven by the love I felt for my grandparents and the warmth and love that they showered on us during the holidays and most importantly, during our Sunday visits to their home and dinner table. One of my fondest childhood memories was visiting my Grandfather Pete's truck farm on Linden Boulevard. During WWII the government encouraged people to grow Victory Farms in their own backyards. An expanded program was truck farming where citizens grew fruits and vegetables for their own consumption and for sale from their trucks or pushcarts. My grandfather had a small farm on the outskirts of Brooklyn. He would take me there to help him plant and harvest his small crop. The fun part of the adventure for an eight to ten year old was lunch. He would pluck some ripe tomatoes and cucumbers from their resting places, slice them into small portions, add provolone and a loaf of Italian sesame seeded bread to our plates, pour some virgin olive oil on top of our feast and voila!! A meal for kings. It was pleasantly washed down with his homemade Italian bitter red wine.

As Seventh Day Adventists, we were not supposed to believe in Christmas Day. According to their religious beliefs December 25 was not when Christ was born. Instead they celebrated his birth everyday. . . . Hence, we had no tree or presents at my house, much to the disappointment of everyone in our immediate family. As a matter of fact, we never had birthday parties or received presents for that occasion, as they were also thought to be insignificant and a waste of money. After Grandpa Pete's funeral, my father decided that we would move in with my grandmother Tootsie on Liberty Avenue, which was only a few blocks from my birthplace; my sister Mae decided otherwise and moved in with my brother Vic and Sister-in-law Rose. I couldn't believe that we were returning to a neighborhood and life that I was unhappy with and was trying to break away from. It meant shoveling coal into stoves again, sleeping on a cot in an alcove with no privacy, living in a neighborhood where the predominant language was Italian, and where I seemed to have very little in common with other boys my age. I felt as if I was trapped, and started looking for a way out of a life that seemed to keep me in bondage. Having served in the National Guard made me consider joining the army to break away from the rut I was in, but providence had something else in mind for me. My turning point came when my friend Paul Maggio and I passed an enlistment center for the United States Air Force on Sutter Avenue. The center was quite a distance from where we lived and luckily near the Pitkin Movie Theater that we were attending that day. After several interviews with the sergeant in charge, we were accepted into the military, and another major turning point in my life became a reality. I found an escape route out of my environment and the restricted existence that was in store for me if I remained.

Free, Free, Free at last. I was on a train to Sampson Air Force Base in upstate New York, near the City of Geneva for basic training, and the beginning of a new life at age 18, far away from all the physical and mental restraints of my past. My mind was set on flying around the world in sophisticated jet planes, discovering new exciting destinations and meeting exotic people. I also expected that basic training would be a physical event; marching, drilling, gun practice and lots of saluting. All of the above were correct, what I didn't expect was spending a considerable amount of time in classrooms. I found myself in a learning environment with blackboards, screeching chalk sounds, movie projector demonstrations and endless lectures about surviving on the battle field, and the importance of the "Military Code of Honor," which we had to commit to memory, and had endless tests on its meaning. The classroom atmosphere I so willingly ran from, captured my attention, and in time, my passion. I was reading, writing, and learning to get along with others in a combined effort to better our chances of survival in the Korean War and also hopefully, in making us better human beings.

Not all major decisions result in turning points, many help us stay our course so that we can eventually take roads that will lead to our final destination. Some decisions help us to avoid turns that might lead us away from our destined course; one such incident happened while I was in boot camp. My drill instructor, Sgt. Fargo asked me to become his assistant because I had previous military experience in the National Guard. The idea of being in charge of my flight was tempting, but after much thought, I turned down the offer even though it would have given me my first stripe and an increase in pay prior to finishing basic training. If I would have taken his offer chances are my life as it is today would not exist. The promotion would have resulted in my remaining at Sampson Air Force Base for a minimum of two years as an instructor, and heaven only knows if I would have had the opportunity for additional schooling with the prospect of learning a trade.

After completing three months of basic training, I waited for my orders that would tell me where and what my next duty assignment would be, and most importantly, what further training I was going to need to fulfill my purpose in the Air Force. Other people were making a decision as to what direction my life was going to point, and I was excited at the prospect of actually getting training that could lead to a good job in the future. My orders arrived and outlined my duties for the next four months; I was to proceed to Francis E. Warren Air Force Base in Cheyenne, Wyoming and report to the Communication Center to begin training as a Communication Specialist. There it was, a decision made by others that would impact the rest of my life. An involuntary turning point, hopefully for the better, that would take me out of the "Blue Color" workforce and mentality, and into a white collared administrative field.

My transportation to Cheyenne was a C-54 Skymaster four-engine-troop carrier. As I previously discussed, we had to force land in Omaha, Nebraska due to heavy ice formations on the wings and fuselage. The sudden loss of altitude in the unpressurized craft caused my ears to pop, which resulted in a severe loss of hearing in my right ear. It was some time before I realized that the ringing in my ear was the aftereffect of the loss. The loss qualified me as a disabled veteran and additional financial benefits would become available for attending school after my four year military enlistment ended, this was not a turning point in my life, but it was one of the circumstances that enabled and encouraged me, after my honorable discharge, to give college a try. There is no doubt in my mind, that if I didn't receive the additional financial aid, I would not have been able to attend Long Island University. So we have an act of providence happening that would be instrumental in my making a major voluntary turn in my life, and put my future on a purposeful path. I got through communication training without any academic problems, but I did have some minor 18-year-old boy discipline situations that almost ended my military career. Fortunately my friends and I had an understanding commanding officer who straightened us out quickly by having us pull K.P. (Kitchen Patrol) duty that included washing and waxing the homogenous dining floors in the various mess halls after class and on weekends for a whole month. Losing our passes was the right punishment for our teenage misbehavior; we quickly learned to toe-the-line and obey our superiors' orders and to abide by the "Military Code of Conduct."

After graduating as a Communications Specialist, I returned to my home on Liberty Avenue in Brooklyn. I enjoyed seeing my family, eating good home cooked meals made with loving care by Grandma Tootsie, my sister Anne and my sister-in-law Rose. When my furlough ended I was glad to leave as I was getting impatient and anxious to meet with the men in my flight in Oakland, California. I boarded the cross-country train in Manhattan and travelled 3,000 boring miles, swearing that I would never again take a long distance trip on a train. Finally arriving at my destination at the Naval Station in Oakland, felt like a homecoming. All of my buddies were there waiting for overseas orders directing them to their destinations. Our orders came; we were assigned to Seoul, Korea, by way of a troop ship, the USS General J.C. Breckinridge. Just before we were to ship out, I came down with a case of acute appendicitis and was rushed to the operating room for the removal of the elongated infected organ. I was given anesthesia and was allowed to watch the operation from the reflection of the overhead mirrors. They showed me the removed greenish finger sized part just before I passed out on the operating table from the sight of the former ugly member of my body.

I spent two weeks in the naval hospital and missed shipping out with the men in my flight. The event certainly resulted in an involuntary turning point. Providence dictated that my destination would not be to the war zone in Korea, but to Japan and eventually to my quarters at the New Kaijo Building, and my work stations in the Meiji Building, and finally the Imperial Palace as a liaison between the military and the Japanese working at their communication center. As one turning point leads to another, so it was with my missing the boat and ending up in Japan where I met Major Johnson, my commanding officer. He liked my work ethics and thought I had potential to better myself, so he took me under his wings and politely coerced me into finishing high school by taking the necessary courses of the United States Armed Forces Institute (USAFI), and then taking the tests required to get a High School General Equivalency Diploma (GED). It took a couple of years before I would accomplish that important turning point, but with the GED under my arm and the financial benefits available to me as a disabled veteran, many doors opened; all I had to do was figure out which one I should walk through. In the meantime, I spent two years in Japan working with my fellow airmen and my Japanese counterparts, learning how to conduct myself like a responsible adult. Before leaving Japan, an event occurred that could have changed the path leading to the person I am today. I was offered a job by a Japanese electronics company as a communication coordinator; it entailed training their employees in our latest communication technology and procedures. A $2,000 sign-on bonus, which was almost a year's salary for me at that time, a nice apartment, and a plush office in downtown Tokyo were very tempting for a 21-year old from Brooklyn. If I accepted, they would make arrangements with the Air Force to extend my tour of duty in Tokyo until I was discharged, which was more than a year away. In addition, the military would arrange for me to attend advanced schooling in communication technology. The bonus would have been paid to me at the signing of an employment contract for five years. The temptation was great, but the picture of Grandma Tootsie sitting in front of our current house on Montauk Avenue in her rose garden, the prospect of having my own room with a real bed, and the call from her delicious Italian sauce and meatballs was too much for me to resist, so I turned down an offer that would have detoured me to a different path in my life, far away from the one that I ended up traveling to get to my final destination. Some of my buddies took the electronic company's offer. The inducement they all had in common was that they all planned on marrying Japanese women and remain in that country. The inviting picture of Grandma Tootsie and my nephews Louis Ambrico and Joseph Bivona posing in her rose garden follows:

Leaving Tokyo was not an easy decision; I had many friends in my Air Force group and in the Imperial Palace. For the first time in my life I was comfortable with a job and the people that I came into contact with every day. I was a sergeant and respected by enlisted men as well as the officers that were part of our group. One of my main concerns was duplicating those conditions back in the States where I would have to begin getting used to my new work surroundings and developing new friendships. But I made up my mind to return to the good old U.S.A., so I packed my bags and headed for Yokohama Naval Base and boarded the faithful old gray lady, the USS General J.C. Breckinridge. The two week voyage to Oakland Naval Station in California was unexpectedly calm, the seas were flat, and the wind pushed us to our destination without incident. The trip gave me lots of time to think about the future and what I was going to do with the rest of my life. The easiest way to determine what kind of a person one wants to become is to look around and see if there is anyone in your life or someone that you've met along your journey that you would like to imitate. After tossing and turning and weighing my options, the one name that kept coming to the surface was Major Johnson, my former commanding officer in Tokyo. The main problem with trying to clone him was that he was a college graduate and I still hadn't finished the required courses to apply for the GED tests. Even if I succeeded in getting my GED, it would be an incredibly long and almost impossible task to match his educational background and his accomplishments.

Oakland Naval Station hadn't changed one iota since my last visit two years before. The only change was me. I wasn't going to take the slow train back home, so I headed straight to the airport, which was befitting a member of the United States Air Force, and boarded the Boeing B-377 Stratocruiser for my flight to LaGuardia Airport, which was only a half an hour from my new home on Montauk Avenue in the East New York section of Brooklyn.

Our new home was not a turning point in my life, but it became instrumental in a major decision that I would have to face when it was time for me to consider whether or not to remain in the Air Force or return to civilian life. Seeing my new home and spending a month with my family, after being away for over two-years, was one of the most memorable events in my life. Grandma Tootsie looked the same and couldn't stop hugging and kissing me everyday during my furlough. My father was a little grayer around the temples, but still looked the same; the noticeable difference was that his Italian accent seemed to have gotten more pronounced. My brother Vic remained his old lovable ornery self and still looked the same as when I saw him two years ago. My sisters Anne, Mae and Rose were more beautiful than I remembered. . . .

I had an opportunity to live at home while serving my remaining time in the military, with a nice off-base allowance for travel, and room and board, which I paid my father to cover my living expenses. Living on Montauk Avenue, while working at Mitchel Field, gave me first-hand experience of what it would be like to return to civilian life, if I chose to do so. It was a whole new unexpected experience; I was in a house that was owned by my family, not by a stranger; I had my own room with lots of privacy, and most importantly, I was surrounded by my whole immediate family. We all lived on the same street for the first time in our lives, from Grandma Tootsie down to my youngest nieces and nephews. Living in such close proximity made our family a close unit and there wasn't any occasion, such as birthdays, confirmations, graduations and sickness that we all weren't involved in. Our family bond was so strong that even after my brother and sisters moved from Montauk Avenue, we all ended up on Long Island, not too far from each other.

After buying my most recent car, I returned to my old neighborhood on Pitkin Avenue, where I spent my formative years, to visit my old haunts and friends. Seeing my onetime buddies hanging around the street corners like lampposts and fire hydrants, in exactly the same positions and discussing the same topics as two years ago, convinced me that sharing their life styles was not what I wanted for my future. The experience was not a turning point, but the picture of that scene became imbedded in my mind, so when making future decisions as to what direction I wanted to travel, that image was always ready to remind me what direction I didn't want to travel.

After spending over a year living at home and traveling to Mitchel Field, my four year enlistment ended, and hence the next major turning point in my life. I was offered a promotion to staff sergeant (four stripes), a $2,500 reenlistment bonus and a guarantee that I would be stationed at the same airbase for at least two years. In addition I would have to move permanently to the airbase and take on the supervisory position at our communications center. The bonus was tempting, the increase in salary from the promotion was also attractive, but I couldn't visualize a future any different than the present if I took their offer and reenlisted for another four years, with the possibility of staying on until retiring in 20-years. It seemed to be a dead-end-road with no prospect for a more enlightening life. So I turned down the offer and became a civilian with a trade in communications, a recently obtained GED certificate and a nice sum of money in the bank. I was in quite a different situation from four years earlier when I escaped my environment and joined the Air Force.

For the first time in my life, I had the potential to become a better person financially and as a human being.

I loved living in our new home and being surrounded by my family. As a bonus, my father and I were getting along pretty well, he stopped preaching to me, which cut down on the friction between us. He was even receptive to getting a telephone (our first phone), and a television set (our first TV set) if I lived at home. What else could a body want? I had my own room, which I painted dark brown with light trim, without any complaint from my father, but lots of negative head shaking from my brother and sisters; a new record player to play my Elvis and Fats Domino 45 and 78 records on, a telephone and a colored television set. I felt as if I died and went to heaven. . . .

After working at a couple of jobs that didn't suit my personality, I accidentally bumped into an old friend of mine in Manhattan at the Palladium Dance Hall, which was one of the most popular singles spots in the city. Arnie, who was a couple of years older than me, was attending New York University (NYU) majoring in physical education with the hope of becoming a baseball coach. He spent four years in the United States Navy, and like me, was able to get his GED while in the military. Well, a light-bulb went off in my head, if he could do it, why not me? After contacting the Veterans Administration and filling out an abundance of documents and then taking aptitude tests, I was given a choice of attending any of the universities or colleges in the metropolitan area. I looked at a map of the city and determined that Long Island University was a short subway ride from where I lived, about 30-minutes. I applied and was accepted as an accounting major. My chance meeting with Arnie lead to one of the most significant turning points in my life. Although I didn't plan on staying at the college for more than a year, I so enjoyed the challenge that I remained to get my Bachelor of Science, with an accounting major and economics minor. I must say my father's cooperation and encouragement was instrumental in my continuing with my studies since I really didn't have enough money to sustain myself at the university, his support was paramount. He wasn't able to give me any money, but I was able to live in his home and eat well throughout my college years at very little cost to me.

The flow of information from subjects like English literature, commercial law, accounting, economics, organic chemistry, mathematics, merchandising, advertising, executive leadership, speech, psychology, philosophy and many other topics, forced the portal of my mind wide open. I received the data with excitement and a passion to absorb as much as I possibly could. I must give credit to many of my professors who encouraged me with constructive criticism and often with praise. If it weren't for their optimism and caring attitudes, it's doubtful if I would have continued with my studies after the first year. I was also fortunate to have been befriended by some very special fellow students. If it wasn't for my friend Benny who I met in the remedial algebra class that was required for me to remain at the university, I would never have passed the "no credit" course. Benny had to take the course because he failed it on the entrance examination, and although he was a high school graduate he didn't have the necessary grades in algebra to enter the university without taking the make-up course. He was proficient in the rudiments, but was weak in logic. I was strong in logic but weak in the fundamentals of equations and formulas. After a week, we had our first test, I received a zero he received 100. The grades were posted and I was not only embarrassed but I was in a lot of trouble, if I didn't pass this course, I was out. . . .

Benny saw my grade and asked to see my test paper. He told me that he could help me as my problem was an easy one to correct. Due to my never having taken the course in high school, I didn't understand the basics, such as two pluses equal a plus, and two minuses also equal a plus. I sucked up the information, and within a month I was getting passing grades. Unfortunately Benny was not, as he had lots of trouble with logic, which I helped him with so he could pass the course, which he did. Talk about providence, if I hadn't met him my whole life without a college education would have gone in a different direction. I can hear all those doors of opportunity closing even today; slam-slam-slam. . . .

At the age of 22 I was one of the oldest freshmen attending the university. I seemed to attract many of the younger 18 and 19 year-olds and sort of became their older brother and mentor. One in particular, my friend Gene, came from a wealthy family but was more interested in playing around with girls and drinking than in studying. In time he straightened out his priorities and graduated alongside me. He taught me to play chess, at which I could never beat him, but more importantly he taught me that "A penny wasted is forever gone," and "A fool and his gold are soon parted." He spent money as if it was going out of style and eventually had his generous allowance stopped by his parents. There were times that I actually had to lend him money. It took lots of coaching and lectures by me to get him on the right path. That experience would come to mind many times in my life when making financial decisions. Earning and spending money is not an inherent right but a privilege, and should not be taken lightly, unless losing it and self destruction is in one's plans.

I had many professors that took time to guide me along the way. In my business studies there were many, especially Professor Philip Wolitzer, who eventually became the chairman of the Accounting Department. He taught my first accounting class which was a complete puzzlement to me. Fortunately the make-up of his grading system included completed homework, which I always handed in neatly and timely. So when figuring my grades, which initially were not very good, he added in my good homework efforts, which allowed me to squeak by my first accounting course with a passing grade. Professor Wolitzer would go on to become a renowned scholar, receiving such illustrious awards as, "Outstanding Educator of America" and was the recipient of the New York State Society of Certified Public Accountant's 2002-2003 Hall of Fame Award for "The prominence he had attained in his professional career." A wing of the LIU Brooklyn Campus, "The Philip Wolitzer Complex," which is a state-of-the-art facility for accounting students, was named in his honor. I was fortunate to be the guest speaker and to share in the ribbon cutting ceremony along side him at its opening, which also included the Michael Bivona Conference Study Classroom. A picture of that event follows:

A professor in the liberal arts department was very instrumental in my becoming passionate about writing and literature. As a freshman, I was unsure of getting through the first year; especially troublesome was my fear of English courses. I passed the "no credit" remedial English course with lots of stress and strain, and was not looking forward to taking the required college English courses in my sophomore year. My main problem was spelling and grammar. Comprehension came pretty easy, but the fundamentals of the language gave me much grief. I used to carry a dictionary with me so I could readily look up words that I wasn't familiar with or couldn't spell. My instructor in English 101 was Professor Joseph Friedman. He had a sophisticated approach for teaching the course; spelling and grammar were important but not as significant as composition. He said "Spelling and grammar would come with practice, but it was the writing and comprehension that would be more useful in our everyday lives." So he allowed us to have dictionaries at our sides when taking writing tests, just as we would if writing outside the classroom; his emphasis was on our developing writing skills. He was a popular writer and editor, and founder of Venture Magazine; he brought an abundance of knowledge and skill of the English language to the classroom. He was made to order for me, I had a dictionary at my side when writing our weekly essays, which helped with my spelling problem and grammar; the creative writing I hoped would come with practice. It was his encouragement that got me interested and eventually passionate about writing. Two of his critiques of my essays follow:

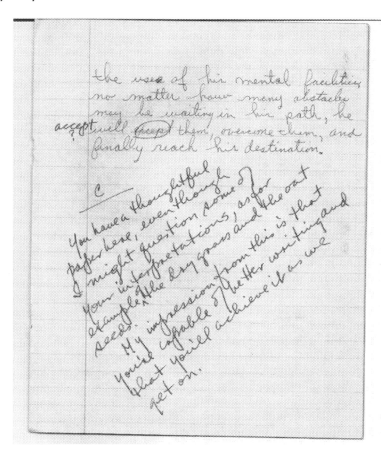

Student's Name...Michael Bivona

Course No. and Section...ENG 1

Instructor's Name...PROF FRIEDMAN

Date Submitted...3/18/58

Date Revised...

Title of Theme...MY FRIEND LUCKY

B+

You have a few assorted writing errors, but you've written an entertaining and thoroughly interesting piece here. You're developing a skillful style, which gives all your work a craftsman's touch.

You might have pushed this to an A if you had shown more of al. Although we do recall people in terms of a dominant characteristic, there are supporting minor elements which help expose the rounded man.

My first essay received a "C" but he wrote, "You have a thoughtful paper here, even though I might question some of your interpretations. . . . My impression from this is that you're capable of better writing and that you'll achieve it as we get on." I almost passed out when I read his generous remarks. He saw a possibility of my being good at a subject that was almost foreign to me, and that I dreaded because I missed high school and didn't have the knowledge or understanding of the basics of the English language. It is not difficult to determine from the above writing that I had a terrible handwriting. After seeing his critique I decided that not only would I pay attention to his studies and advice, but I also began to drill myself in writing the alphabet in block letters and then in longhand, until it became what I thought was an acceptable presentation of English penmanship. My second essay got me a shocking "B+" and sent me on a quest to learn as much as I could about the strange world of English reading and writing. His comments stated, "You have a few assorted writing errors, but you've written an entertaining and thoroughly interesting piece here. You're developing a skillful style, which gives all of your work a craftsman's touch. You might have pushed this to an 'A' . . . ." Well, after that I was hooked on writing. I received many B pluses and an occasional "A" on my essays, my final grade for the course was my first "A." Miracle of miracles, the somewhat illiterate kid from Brooklyn had a chance of completing a college education now that his most dreaded and difficult subject was no longer a threat. I went on to become an editor and writer for the accounting newsletter "Footnote" and "Tomorrow's Managers," and wrote many articles for other university publications. This experience was not a turning point as such, but an event that would allow me to use my new found talent to advance myself in business and in my personal life, and gave me an enormous boost in confidence. I loved the English courses so much that as electives I chose "Shakespearean Literature," and "Creative Writing." I loved the "Creative Writing" course but the "Shakespearean Literature" course was a mistake. It required lots of research and studying, and demanded lots of my precious time, which could have been put to better use by my taking easier courses such as

Advertising or Marketing, which would have been more conducive to my business major.

Things began to move very quickly. In my junior year I was asked to work in the Accounting Department to assist the professors with research and other tasks, such as preparing and grading accounting tests. In those days copying machines were not readily available, and those that were on hand were very clumsy to use and didn't produce clear copies, so my typing skills came in handy when researching and outlining topics that the professors wanted me to investigate and report on. In addition, I was asked to run for the office of President of the Accounting Society, which was a very prestigious position, with a possible opportunity for getting into a master's degree program with a stipend. I couldn't believe all of the wonderful opportunities that were becoming available to me. In addition to becoming the president of the Accounting Society, I was already president of the Veterans Club, which I helped establish for the many Korean War veterans that were attending the university and felt out of place socializing with the younger teenage students. As president of the society, I was responsible for supervising and overseeing the "Accounting Seminar" and "Accounting Footnote" publications, in addition to assisting students in our Tutoring Program, which I helped initiate. The program was based on the military's "Buddy System," where senior servicemen assisted recruits in survival techniques in time of war. Being the director of the tutoring program was very gratifying. Witnessing its inception and growth, and seeing how beneficial it was to accounting students that needed assistance with their studies, was instrumental in my "Pay it forward" attitude that stayed with me for the rest of my life.

I decided to hasten my exit from the halls of education by taking accelerated courses over the summer months. By doing this I was able to graduate in a little over three years instead of four. My whirlwind experience at the university was heightened when I was offered a stipend to attend graduate school for a master's degree and to continue working in the Accounting Department, with the prospect of eventually teaching at LIU. I gave it much thought; I loved the "halls of wisdom" and the excitement of being part of an educational institution, which a few years earlier was not even a remote possibility for me, but I just didn't see myself as a good educator. My dream was slowly developing, reinforced by the picture of my St. George Hotel experience imbedded in my mind; I saw myself in the future as a captain of industry and a part of the financial "wheel of fortune." So, with heavy heart, I turned down the offer that would have led me on a different road in my life. Imagine, I wouldn't have met my beautiful wife Barbara, I wouldn't have been successful in my many business ventures and worst of all, I would not have had my two fabulous children, Steve and Laurie and my two grandchildren Ian and Katie. My decision was not a turning point, but it did keep me on the track that would lead to my eventual destination as a business entrepreneur, a husband to Barbara, and the father of Steve and Laurie. If I had taken the offer to remain at the university, it would have resulted in one of the major turning points in my life and I most certainly would not be the person I am today.

A letter nominating me for "Outstanding Student," sort of outlines my situation right before graduating from Long Island University. A copy of the letter and picture of me in my year book for 1960 follows:

Michael Bivona
360 Montauk Avenue, Brooklyn
Accounting
Co-ordinating Committee of College
of Business Administration, Treasurer;
Accounting Society, President; Veterans' Club, President.

ACCOUNTING SOCIETY
LONG ISLAND UNIVERSITY
BROOKLYN 1, NEW YORK

April 20, 1960

Director of Student Affairs:

In reference to your letter dated April 8, 1960 for the nomination of
outstanding students in this Society for University Service Awards;
the following is a list of those students who have contributed their
time and effort to the University and their fellow peers:

Michael Bivona
360 Montauk Ave
Brooklyn 8, New York

SPECIFICATIONS:

President Accounting Society (current)
President Veteran's Club 1958-1959
Treasurer College of Business Administration Co-ordinating Committee
Director of College Business Administration Christmas Party 1959
Director of Accounting Tutoring System for undergraduates
Co-Director of College of Business Administration Picnic May 1, 1960
Essayist of "Accounting as a Tool of Management" appearing in MODERN MANAGEMENT.
    C.B.A. 1960
Writer of articles appearing in Accounting "Footnote" 1960

Robert Wise
314 Brighton Beach Ave
Bklyn, New York

SPECIFICATIONS:

Editor-in-Chief of Accounting "Footnote"
Editor-in-Chief of Accounting Seminar

Wearing my cap and gown, I walked up to the stage at the Brooklyn
Paramount Theater to receive my Bachelor of Science Degree and my
Outstanding Service Medal. My father, brother and sisters were looking
on and bursting with pride as my name was called. I on the other hand,
was in a state-of-shock and disbelief that I was receiving a document
that attested to the fact that I had received a college education, without
ever attending high school. The 4,000-plus seat theater was filled to
the rafters with relatives and friends all brimming with delight that
their loved ones were in the procession of scholars wearing their unique
colored robes that reflected which school they were graduating from.
When the last name was called and the audience settled down, the
2,000 piped Wurlitzer organ, the second largest in the world, played
"You'll Never Walk Alone." The words to the song described perfectly
the feeling that I had at that moment; I was ready to conqueror the
world, and sang those appropriately touching words along with my
fellow graduates:

"When you walk through a storm, hold your head
up high and don't be afraid of the dark.

At the end of the storm there's a golden sky
and the sweet silver song of a lark.

Walk on through the wind, walk on through the rain
though your dreams be tossed and blown.

Walk on, walk on with hope in your heart
and you'll never walk alone."

Saying goodbye to some of the professors that I had worked closely with, and befriended, was not an easy task. Fortunately I stayed in contact with some of them, especially Professor Philip Wolitzer who remains my mentor and dear friend till this day. There was no question in my mind what I would be doing for the next three years. To obtain a Certified Public Accounting license required that I serve a three year apprenticeship with a public accounting firm in preparation for taking the New York State Certified Public Accounting Examination. All of the major turning points and many of the distractions that could have changed my future led me to the road that I recognized was my course in life. My goal was to become a licensed accountant and then find a job in the airline industry traveling around the world, and possibly becoming another Howard Hughes. I spent the next three years working for the accounting firm of David B. Jacobs & Co. at 19 Rector Street in Manhattan. They specialized in servicing large private companies, such as Pepperidge Farms, prior to its merger with Campbell Soup. We also had such illustrious clients as Richard Rogers and David Rockefeller. So I was introduced into the world of privately owned large businesses, and dealt with some of the personalities that were responsible for the success of their companies. In the meantime, my home life was going very well. My brother Vic and my sister-in-law Rose added three more children to their household, Grace, Carl and Michael. My father married a sweet lady that he knew from his church, Mary DiAngelo; so I had three more children living above me for a total of five, and one other person living with me and my father. My sister Mae married her childhood friend, Sal Curti, and moved a couple of blocks from us; in time they added two children to our family, Peter and Paulette. We were all living in close proximity to each other and enjoyed sharing holidays, picnics, and birthdays, which seemed to be on the average of every month. The vitality of our growing and prosperous family could be felt around the dinner tables and at our various holidays and celebrations.

In the late1950s and early1960s a new term for travelers became popular, "Jet Set." It described an international social group of wealthy people, organizing and participating in around the world social activities that were not available to the average person because it was too expensive to fly the new introduction to air flight; jet planes. When Boeing Aircraft developed the 707 jet aircraft, and it became a safe commercial way to travel at reasonable prices, the door opened for the average person to join the ranks of the "Jet Setters." A copy of the Boeing 707 follows:

I was not about to let an opportunity to fly in a jet plane pass me by, so my friend and I booked a flight on an American Airlines Boeing 707 to El Paso, Texas, where we planned on taking a bus into Mexico to our final destination, Mexico City. I was not only the first one in my family to fly in a jet plane, but most of my friends and neighbors who hadn't had the experience yet, thought I was crazy. Crazy or not we boarded the silver bullet at JFK airport and were soon on our way to El Paso. The shiny beauty was 152 feet long, 42 feet high with a wing span of 142 feet. It carried over 180 passengers in comfortable extra wide seats, with lots of leg room to stretch out when in a reclining position. Everything in the plane was bright-shiny-new with the aroma that goes along with new leather, cloth and carpeting. We traveled at the unthinkable speed of 500-miles per hour at an unimaginable cruising altitude of 35,000 feet. We flew over 2,100 miles in a little over four hours, a big difference from my last flight from California to New York which took 10 hours on a four engine propeller plane. The ease in which that flight delivered its passengers in comfort and safety, was my introduction to becoming an avid traveler, which is still a part of my persona today. Barbara and I travel as much as we can; as a matter of fact I just published a book "Dancing Around the World with Mike and Barbara Bivona." On April 10, 2010 we had a book signing and presentation of the book at Gold Coast Ballroom in Coconut Creek, Florida. We presented a copy of the book to Karina Smirnoff who is one of the professionals on the reality show "Dancing With the Stars." There are two great pictures in the book of her dancing with Louie van Amstel, also a star on the show, at the Suburban Center in Wantagh, New York, which Barbara and I attended. A copy of the front and back cover of the soft covered book follows with a picture of Karina's performance card and also a picture of her with me and Barbara:

MICHAEL BIVONA

From Buenos Aires to Paris to New Orleans, Mike and Barbara Bivona have traveled and danced throughout the world. And in this memoir and travelogue, these two dance aficionados share their adventures and experiences.

Ballroom dancers for more than twenty years, the Bivonas have traveled extensively while honing their dancing skills and meeting fellow dancers. Dancing Around the World with Mike and Barbara Bivona provides detailed accounts of their experiences in Argentina, Paris, Hawaii, Italy, the Catskill Mountains of New York, the Caribbean, and South Florida, as well as other destinations. This account not only includes dancing details, but also shares the history and flavor of the exciting locales they have visited.

Augmented with photographs, Dancing Around the World with Mike and Barbara Bivona also includes background information on the art of ballroom dancing, a few dance lessons, biographies of select dancers who have performed on the television show Dancing with the Stars, current ballroom dancing philosophy, and information about the intellectual benefits gained from dancing.

• •

MIKE BIVONA is a tango aficionado, book collector, writer, philanthropist, and traveler. He and his wife, Barbara, have been ballroom dancers for over twenty years; they are members of USA Dance and Argentine Tango Lovers of Long Island. The Bivonas live in Long Island, New York, and Delray Beach, Florida. Also by author, *"Business Infrastructure in a Computer Environment,"* Vantage Press, NY 2001.

There was an overnight stop-over in El Paso. Since Texas is beef country, I couldn't be happier; for dinner I had a filet mignon steak, second to none, but the real treat was a New York sirloin steak with three sunny-side-up eggs on top, which I had for breakfast. Talk about a cholesterol nightmare, but, nightmare or not, it was the most delicious breakfast that I had ever eaten. Our 1,100-mile Greyhound bus trip began at 8 AM. The three days journey took us to Juarez, Chihuahua, Durango, and many other small towns, and then finally Mexico City. The social shock that I experienced still lives with me today. The larger cities for the most part were clean and thriving, but the smaller towns were rundown with people living in substandard conditions in makeshift houses, many with no roofs, and most with dirt floors. On the trip I witnessed a bullfight in one of the small towns. The matadors were amateurs and had a difficult time fighting the large bulls. Many of the young boys were taken off the battlefield on stretchers, with broken limbs or skulls bashed in by their opponents. That is another Mexican sight that still lives with me, and is responsible for my pacifist attitude toward inhumane cruelty to animals and humans. We

145

were fortunate to have met Americans on the bus trip that we spent the rest of our vacation with. We took in the museums, enjoyed nightclub shows and met lots of the senoritas, who were friendly, and anxious to show us the sights.

When our journey came to an end, we quickly boarded another American Airlines Boeing 707 for our return trip home to New York, It took a little longer to return due to turbulent weather conditions, but the friendly hostesses and the free drinks made the flight home comfortable and a pleasant experience. On the six hour flight back I had lots of time to reflect on what I wanted to do with my life. Things were going well; I was a 27-year old bachelor, had a shiny (not new) car, a great job in Public Accounting, was studying to take the CPA exams, and was actually able to put money aside every week from my generous paycheck. What more could I need?

I considered myself a bona fide "Jet Setter," so the following year I decided to fly to Quebec, Canada on another Boeing 707 jet plane for a ten days summer vacation. After checking with the Automobile Club of New York for the best hotel in Quebec, I chose the "Fairmont Le Chateau Frontenac." Their brochure stated: "Standing high on the bluff overlooking the mighty St. Lawrence River, it is not merely a hotel located in the heart of Old Quebec – it is the heart of the old city." That was just the information I was looking for. I boarded the jet at JFK airport and again was airborne in a jet propelled airplane; I was truly a member of the Jet Set. Looking at the Chateau Frontenac was surreal; it had a reddish brown exterior façade with aged greenish copper roofs, and a turreted castle design connecting a six wing complex that boasted an 18 foot tower that was easily seen from my window in the airplane as we approached the city. The Chateau overlooked the old city and the St. Lawrence River and seemed to act as their guardian. It had to be one of the most beautiful hotels in the world, or one of the most beautiful ones that I had seen up until that time. It had an indoor swimming pool, gym, spa and an outdoor ice-skating rink for winter use. A glass funicular ran down the side of the bluff that deposited guests on the Riverwalk, which was a short walking distance from Old Quebec. The hotel was built in 1893 in the center of Old Quebec; it is 18-stories high with over 600 elegant chateau style rooms and all of the amenities that a five star hotel must feature.

The inside lobby had a deep rich old world mahogany wood look, complemented with antique 19th century large chairs, overstuffed couches, enormous chandeliers, and dark furniture accessories. I settled into my comfortable room that was well decorated with furniture of the same period, including a king sized bed. I spent the first few days sightseeing up and down the mighty St. Lawrence River, stopping off at little fishing villages for lunch, enjoying French cuisine and the beautiful harmonious language that the friendly French-Canadians spoke. The hotel itself featured a five star restaurant that I enjoyed on my first night; that is until I got the bill. I quickly determined that a second meal at the high class establishment was out of the question, as I was on a very strict budget and had to watch how I spent money. I always had a tendency of spending most of my money in the first few days of a vacation and was determined not to do it on my Canadian journey. A memorable tour was visiting Montreal to see "St. Joseph's Oratory of Mount Royal," a Roman Catholic basilica on the northern slope of the mountain in Montreal, Quebec. The basilica is dedicated to Saint Joseph the husband of Mary Mother of Christ, who is credited with all of the miracles performed by Brother Andrea on the site, such as healing the blind, handicapped, ill, etc. On display is a wall covered with thousands of crutches from those who came to the basilica and were healed. A reliquary in the church museum contains the beautified heart of Brother Andrea. The church has one of the highest domes in the world, second only to St. Peter's Cathedral in Rome. There are over 200 steps leading to the entrance which are used by those seeking forgiveness for transgressions or those seeking special favors. It was shocking to see people climbing the steps on their knees, although most of them wore knee pads, but the journey must have been grueling, and hopefully resulted in prayers being answered or sins forgiven.

What captured my attention was the larger than life statuary lined up in the beautiful gardens of the "15-Stations of the Cross." I visited each marble station, refreshing my memory as to their purpose and religious significance. As I studied each sculpture, that seemed to come alive as its meaning rushed into my mind, I was spellbound at the beauty and the warmth of the marble. The white stones became pale flesh as I was drawn into their significance. I spent over two hours visiting:

Station 1 – Jesus is condemned to Death.

Station 2 – Jesus is laden with the Cross.

Station 3 – Jesus falls for the first time under the weight of the cross.

Station 4 – Jesus meets his mother Mary.

Station 5 – Simon of Cyrene helps Jesus carry the cross.

Station 6 – A women wipes Jesus' face.

Station 7 – Jesus falls a second time.

Station 8 – Jesus comforts the women of Jerusalem.

Station 9 – Jesus falls a third time.

Station 10 – Jesus is stripped of his garments.

Station 11 – Jesus is nailed to the cross.

Station 12 – Jesus dies on the cross.

Station 13 – Jesus is taken down from the cross.

Station 14 – Jesus is placed in a tomb.

Station 15 – Jesus is resurrected.

Well, after leaving the sacred grounds with tears in my eyes and stiffness in my throat, I couldn't believe how deeply my religious upbringing was still imbedded in me. All of my Bible studies about Jesus that I thought I had forgotten came rushing back into my mind and heart with an unexpected emotional rush.

I began to run out of money while staying at the Chateau, which wasn't a big surprise to me. My credit card limit wasn't enough to keep me in the luxury hotel for the remainder of the trip, so I asked the concierge Pierre if there was a less expensive hotel in the old city that I could spend the rest of my vacation at. He recommended a small hotel in town by the name of Louis . . . , I don't recall the exact name, but it had about 20 rooms and was built and decorated like a French countryside inn; very quaint with an "At home feeling." I settled in and was relieved that there was enough credit on my card and enough remaining cash in my pocket to continue my vacation in style at the less expensive inn. At breakfast the next morning I noticed a dozen or so beautiful girls enjoying their meals, the only problem was that I was the only guy in the dining room. A couple of friendly beauties came over to my table and asked if they could join me. What a question to ask a 27 year old bachelor: I immediately said yes. Gennette and Mimi both spoke English with very heavy French accents, which really fascinated me, as it gave me the feeling that I was in France. Gennette was a model and Mimi an aspiring actress. It seemed that I hit a pot of gold; all the residents were either models or actresses. I spent the remaining few days enjoying the company of the friendly girls who were thrilled to have someone to practice their English with. They even took me sightseeing and introduced me to the owners of many small restaurants in the city, where I was treated as a long lost relative, and showered with many homemade meals and great French wines. We were all short of cash, so we spent lots of time at the hotel playing cards, especially poker, and pick-up-sticks. The temptation to call my boss and family in New York and tell them that I was relocating to Old Quebec was very great, but I knew that all good things must come to an end. So, I said my goodbyes at the going away party that the girls threw for me, and gave each of them hugs and kisses with promises of returning to them with more money in my pocket. The next morning I dragged myself to the airport for my return flight back home to my reality. I must say that looking back at that wonderful experience certainly reinforced my love for traveling, and my willingness to open new doors to see what adventure lies beyond. The experience was another reinforcement on my journey through life, a reinforcement that encouraged traveling and experimenting with the unknown.

My next turning point was soon looking me in the eyes at the offices of Rugoff Theaters at 1270 Avenue of the Americas, which was adjacent to Radio City Music Hall and part of the Rockefeller Plaza Complex. A novel Xmas ornament setting that was displayed at Gold Coast Ballroom, which is located in Coconut Creek, Florida, of Radio City Music Hall and 1270 Avenue of the America's buildings follows:

On the 17th floor sat the beautiful Barbara Selden, who worked in Rugoff Theater's management department. Her gleaming smile captivated me, and I quickly asked her out for a luncheon date. Mr. Rugoff was one of the first to present art movies in New York City, and showed great first run exclusive movies, such as, GIGI and Japanese art films, many of which played in two theaters simultaneously. Their 15 movie houses, which included some of the first multiplex theaters in the metropolitan area, kept Barbara busy keeping track of their financial records. My job as an auditor was to keep track of what Barbara was doing, which I did very well, during and after work hours. We courted for two years and at age 30 I asked her to be my bride. Getting married wasn't a turning point in my life, but meeting my perfect mate kept me on the course that I had chosen. It also enhanced the possibility of my dreams becoming a success, and having a wonderful family and a house in the suburbs. Our wedding picture toasting our success follows. On the left are Charles and Frances Selden, in the middle beautiful Barbara Bivona and handsome moi, and on the right my father's new wife Mary DiAngelo and my Dad Luciano Joseph Bivona:

Around the time Barbara and I married, the rest of my family was in a state-of-flux; my sister Anne and family moved to a place called Deer Park on Long Island. It took forever to get there from Brooklyn by car; we all thought that it was a bad move for them, until my brother and his family moved a few blocks from her, leaving me and my father alone in Brooklyn.

My sister Mae and her family had already moved to Oceanside, a little town on Long Island, which was only 20 minutes from Brooklyn. My father and Vic sold their two-family house on Montauk Avenue. My father moved to another location in that borough called Bensonhurst, which was very close to the Verrazano Bridge and walking distance to his church. I moved into Barbara's apartment on Flatbush Avenue in 1964. The avenue was famous for the Brooklyn Dodger's Ebbets Field baseball stadium, the Brooklyn Botanical Gardens, and the many shops and restaurants along the large avenue. A nice feature was that it was around the corner from Prospect Park and the Rutland Road subway station, which got us into Manhattan to where we were both working at that time, in about ½ an hour. Prospect Park has to be seen to be believed. It wasn't quite as large as Central Park in Manhattan, but it had a large lake with rowboats for rent, horseback riding, a first class zoo and lots of grass which was put to good use by the many picnic blankets scattered around the area. The apartment building we lived in had a security guard station at the front door, an underground garage, and was only a few years old. Our apartment was "L" shaped, but had a nice sized combination living and dining room, a small kitchen, an alcove bedroom and a great bathroom with a tub and a wonderful shower, which I put to good use often; we even had an air conditioning unit in our window. The only problem was that we were on the ground floor of a 17-story building, and when the subway train passed our window, the rooms rocked and rolled. So, as soon as our lease was up, we moved to Menlo Park, New Jersey, where for $140.00 a month we rented a relatively new townhouse with an eat-in-kitchen, dining area, living room, full bedroom, central air conditioning and a terrace. We took a bus into Manhattan every day to get to our jobs. Our bus stop was only a couple of blocks from where we lived, which made traveling very convenient. We looked forward to the comfortable air conditioned bus ride into the city every day, enjoying our coffee, newspaper and daily naps. Menlo Park, which was the former site of Thomas Edison's laboratory, was only a short car ride from where my father lived in Brooklyn; he had become very ill with fibrosis of the lungs, so we visited him often, and enjoyed relaxing and devouring Mary's Italian cooking. One of their remaining loves was spending a couple of weeks of the summer in the Catskill Mountains' retreat of their church, enjoying the religious services and the camaraderie of their church members. Driving them to that beautiful area of upstate New York, made Barbara and I frequent vacationers of that mountainous area later on in our lives. Taking the Verrazano Bridge into Brooklyn was also a pleasant ride; it was a fairly new bridge and crossing it made us feel as if we were going on a holiday. We bought a new 1965 Malibu Chevrolet which we used as often as we could, so visiting my father by car was like a mini-vacation to us.

While still living on Flatbush Avenue, we decided to take a vacation to Italy, so we took lessons in Italian at Brooklyn College and couldn't wait to make the journey. That is until we saw an 18-foot Crestliner runabout boat at the National Boat Show at the New York City Coliseum. For the same price as the trip to Italy we could buy a new speedboat. We also convinced ourselves that owning a nice pleasure boat was a better investment than a one time trip to Italy; little did we realize that it was the beginning of many boats and the spending of "mucho dinero." So the turn that would put us on a life-long passion for boating began with a red and white 18-foot speedboat named "Big One." From there we kept upsizing, first to a 28-foot Chris Craft, then a 35-foot Christ Craft and finally the boat we now own, our 42-foot Chris Craft, Mikara. A copy of that boat with Barbara, Vic, Rose, Mae, Sal, Anne and Captain Red follows:

With the help of my beautiful wife Barbara, I passed the Certified Public Accounting Examination. The exams consisted of four parts: Law, Accounting Theory, Auditing and Practical Accounting. In those days, I could only sit for Law and Theory first and the other two parts after passing Law and Theory. I originally passed Law and failed Theory, and then I passed Theory and failed Law. Both exams had to be passed simultaneously to receive credit, a strange requirement, which I think has changed. With the help of my wife's drilling me with tax and accounting questions, I did pass all four parts and became a licensed New York Certified Public Accountant. Not a turning point, but an enhancement that reinforced my determination to become a professional accountant, and possibly a captain of industry.

While we lived in New Jersey, my beloved father Luciano Joseph Bivona, who was born on St. Lucy's birthday and hence the name Luciano, passed away at age 74. While living he preferred being called Joe, and would get pleasantly annoyed when I called him Lucy. He preferred his grandfather's and uncle's name, Joe, as it was more Americanized than Luciano. There was no longer any reason for us to remain in New Jersey, so we started looking around for a place on Long Island near my brother and sisters. Around that time, my three year mandatory apprenticeship in public accounting concluded, (I received six months credit for being in the military). I left the public accounting world and entered the private business sector, hoping to become a captain of industry and making lots of money. I worked for several large corporations as a controller; the experience was not to my liking, so I decided that being a captain of industry was not in the cards for me and decided to return to public accounting and go into my own business. Sounds easy? Well one doesn't just hang out a shingle and say "World, here I am." I had to work per diem (on a daily basis) for other accounting firms until I could build my own practice. An opportunity came along during that time that could have changed my life drastically and put me on a road quite different from what I had planned. I worked per diem for an accounting firm that specialized in servicing people in the entertainment field. They had clients, such as, Tony Bennett, Connie Francis, Florence Henderson, and Diana Ross and the Supremes. They had offices in Manhattan and Los Angeles and wanted to open an office in Nashville, Tennessee. They offered me a partnership in their firm and wanted me to scout for an office in that city, and then move there to service their existing and hopefully new clients in that bustling entertainment center. They offered me a huge salary and profit sharing. Barbara and I gave the offer some serious thought, it meant leaving Barbara's aging parents in Brooklyn and my family on Long Island, and relocating to a new location where we would be strangers speaking a slightly different language than the locals. We didn't have any children at that time, but we joked about their growing up with southern accents and their socializing with children of the rich and famous clients that the firm would hopefully have. I finally turned the offer down and instead contracted to build a house in Dix Hills on the border of Deer Park, Long Island just four blocks from Vic and Rose, and eight blocks from my sister Anne. Barbara and I knew in what direction we would like to see our lives move, and with her assistance and good sense, and my hard work, we were traveling on a road we felt comfortable with.

From that point on there were no major turning points in our lives, just human and financial adjustments. We were a married couple, and I was a professional accountant, those facts hopefully wouldn't change. We moved into our newly built three bedroom house that sat in the middle of one-quarter of an acre, on Weymouth Street in 1968. Shortly after we moved our blue eyed, blonde haired, 10½ pound son, Steve was born. A little over a year, Barbara gave birth to our chubby hazel eyed, brown haired, 5-pound 12-ounce daughter Laurie. So our dream of having our own home with two children became a reality. We couldn't be happier. I was only working per diem for other accounting firms when I had the time as my accounting practice was growing at a steady pace. Barbara did all of the typing of my clients' financial statements and my billing, she also kept track of my accounts receivable while attending to two babies. We made a good team, I earned the money, she kept track of it and knew just when it was appropriate to go shopping.

We lived on Weymouth Street for six years when we decided to move to a larger home. It was during the real estate boom on Long Island and we were fortunate to sell our house for almost double the price that we paid, although it took over a year to sell as banks were not giving mortgages easily. When it sold we had two months to find a new place to live. We saw an advertisement in the Sunday New York Times for a house on a court that we were familiar with. We previously looked at a house there and loved it and the neighborhood, the only problem was that it was oil heated. Both Steve and Laurie had chronic allergy problems and owning a home with that kind of a heating system was not an option. The wise accountant that was selling his home on the same court, decided to choose clean burning gas heat when the house was built, due to the fact that his children had the same allergy problems as Steve and Laurie. So providence played its card, and we became the new owners of our home on Broadley Court in Dix Hills; I'm proud to say that for over 36 years it is still our New York home. So in a short time, two voluntary actions on our part, buying a boat and a house in Dix Hills, determined that we would spend our leisure time boating for the rest of our lives, and spend our remaining days living on Broadley Court.

During our first years on Broadley Court, we saw a movie with John Travolta, "Saturday Night Fever." He played the part of Tony Manero dancing with Karen Gorney as Stephanie Mangano. Their Hustle variation startled and excited audiences all over the world. Those wonderful young actors started a dance craze unequalled since the Valentino phenomenon that had him dancing the passionate Tango in silent films and made it a popular dance throughout the world in the early 1900s. Many people started taking Hustle lessons after seeing the movie. We took lessons for a short period of time, but our busy family life and my growing business didn't allow any spare time for that fun sport. We put taking lessons on hold for about ten years when our children were in college and no longer living with us. We continued our dance lessons at "Swing Street Studios" in Farmingdale, with the talented Elektra Underhill. We credit her with our passions for dancing, as her skill, patience and understanding nursed and nurtured us through our many dance lessons. Our first lessons were Tango and Swing. Barbara and I danced together for many years at weddings and other social events, but never got the hang of doing Tango or Swing very well. A problem I had with taking additional lessons was the thought of being criticized by the instructor and, of course, my beloved, an event that went against my macho persona. It took a lot of patience on their part before I learned how to behave myself when given constructive criticism. Our lessons were the beginning of a lifelong love affair with ballroom and social dancing. We still take dancing lessons in New York with Louis Del Prete and in Florida with Brian Smith, our social life in Florida and New York continue to revolve around dancing people and dance venues. It also got us into writing for the Long Island dance publication "Around the Floor." Many of our articles appear in my book "Dancing Around the World with Mike and Barbara Bivona." So while living in Dix Hills, a passion for dancing and writing became an integral part of our lives. A copy of the publications "Around the Floor's About Us" follows:

ABOUT US

"Around The Floor" is the product of a collective non-profit effort on the part of a group of amateur and professional dancers with the mission of sharing "The Magic of the Dance" The feature writers and guest authors listed below have made this magazine possible.

vemilano@suffolk.lib.ny.us   minho1@optonline.net

Vincent Milano, Editor   Adrian Cabral, Publisher

Barbara Bivona   Mike Bivona   Paulette O'Neil   Lorraine and Tony Laudicina   Donna Pardi-D'Andrea

Patti Panebianco

Nancy Ladika   Paul and Maggie Cesare

Dean and Cindy Monaco

My accounting practice was doing well. My nephew Louis Ambrico joined the firm after graduating from C.W. Post University; in time he became a partner, which added another name to our firm of Bivona, Dlugacz and Ambrico, Certified Public Accountants. My sister Anne, Louis' mother, also joined the firm. She was our office manager and was in charge of the bookkeeping functions of our firm and some of our clients; she was also responsible for our computer operations. Our firm was successful in part due to my relationship with various banks and the many attorneys that we had as clients; both referred business our way. Being a member of the "Tax Practitioner's Forum" at C.W. Post University, which was limited to sixty-professionals, and met monthly to discuss the latest tax court rulings, and the New York State Tax Committee with the CPA Society, were also instrumental in my meeting many business contacts that helped our firm to flourish.

After being in public accounting for over 25 years, I was offered part ownership in a client's business, the offer was too good not to consider. We worked out a deal where I would work for three months on a trial basis to see if my prospective partners and I were compatible and comfortable with each other; if successful, I would become a part owner of Manchester Technology, a personal computer enhancer and reseller. The main attraction for me was that it was a computer company servicing the fortune 1,000-companies, and had lots of potential for growth in the budding personal computer (PC) market. I would be the controller in charge of finance and administrative operations with the latest computer technology and equipment at my disposal to assist me in my task of bringing the company into the 21st century. The opportunity came in 1985 when I was 50-years old to possibly become a captain of industry after all, which was my original dream after graduating college.

Beginning a new career was not a turning point but a major adjustment and enhancement to my lifestyle. In the public accounting arena, traveling to clients' places of business was an integral part of the job, so was tax season, which begins January 1ˢᵗ and ends around the end of April. Traveling by car on Long Island and New York City was becoming a stressful and time consuming affair that wasted up to three hours a day of my precious time. Tax season seemed to never end; during that time I would work from early morning till late at night, six and sometime seven days a week. One of the reasons that boating was so precious to our family was that after a busy tax season, a welcomed springtime season began, and signaled that it was time to devote our family efforts to preparing our boat for the summer season of fun and frolic. This gave me an opportunity to spend lots of quality time with Barbara and Steve and Laurie, which was lacking during my busy tax season. We enjoyed preparing the boat for summer operation and the resultant boat trips throughout Long Island and the surrounding area. My new career required that I work from eight-thirty to five-thirty, five days a week. I had 52-weekends free to enjoy my family and I was able to be home for dinner every evening to enjoy Barbara's wonderful cuisine and the happy faces of my children. The change of careers enhanced the quality of my life immeasurably, as well as financially.

At the time of my career change, our accounting firm was located on Broadway in the town of Massapequa, Long Island. I was fortunate to own half of the office building with two attorney friends, Steve Kressel and Joel Rothlein, which made it easy for my nephew Louis to take over my accounting practice without having to relocate. I signed a three year contract with Manchester Technology that turned into an eleven year adventure. I use the word adventure because the time I spent with the company turned out to be the thrill-of-a-lifetime. When I began working with the organization it was a small company with sales of around 20-million dollars a year. Although their growth was solid, the company was administratively and operationally disorganized and on the verge of going out of business. My new partners were experts in sales and merchandising, but they had neither the interest nor the resources to run the organization profitably or efficiently. The fun part of the job was that I had the latest computer technology and equipment at my disposal to assist me in bringing the company to the highest level of administrative and operational efficiency. It took the better part of a year to hire the right people and fire all of the wrong personnel, which was about 1/3 of the employees, but after 12-months the back-office, warehouse, service and transportation departments were all considered state-of-the-art operations. Companies from around the world would visit to see how efficiently the organization ran and to clone our computer and bar coding systems. When I began working there in 1985, personal computer applications and bar coding were just beginning to successfully come onto the business scene. There was a vast difference in the price of a PC compared to a mainframe; the lower prices allowed businesses of every size to take a chance on trying the new technology. We customized PCs for our customers, which allowed them to use similar applications as the larger more expensive mainframes, without investing tens-of-thousands of dollars in expensive equipment. It allowed companies to have PCs on their employees' desks, and in many instances, with our help, have them connected to each other, and where available, to their expensive mainframes, which enhanced sharing information. Those new applications resulted in necessary and valuable tools for organizations' management infrastructure. My first book "Business Infrastructure in a Computer Environment" covers the importance of the technology at that time as it related to management. A copy of the front cover of my book, which my son Steve designed, along with the cover's back page follows:

Within the structure of today's increasingly complex corporate world, author Michael Bivona's *Business Infrastructure: In a Computer Environment* is a blueprint for success.

As technology and finance shape tomorrow's companies, organizational issues become more and more crucial. The author's analysis clearly shows how wise development can translate into increased profits and productivity. The complexities of infrastructure are examined with regard to internal operations, such as customer service departments.

This is a book that is certain to be welcomed by managers and supervisors in large and small firms; and a must for young people starting out in the business world.

Providence would play another important part in our lives. My son Steve decided to attend the State University of New York (SUNY), Albany. So we packed his belongings and drove him to the large campus in upstate New York. After saying our goodbyes, we returned to our hotel, the Ramada Inn, for dinner and a well deserved night's sleep. In the morning we planned on Barbara taking the first leg of our four hour trip back to Long Island and I would then drive the rest of the way. After breakfast we packed our suitcases and were ready to leave, when the "nightmare of all nightmares" happened. Barbara had a seizure and passed out right in front of my eyes. I tried to revive her, but to no avail. I called the manager, he called an ambulance, and in record time she was at Albany Medical Center. The doctors said that the manager's quick actions probably saved Barbara's life. After a cat scan it was determined that an aneurysm (blood vessel) had burst, and sent blood onto her brain. They weren't sure if they could save her. They gave me the odds for survival: one half of all the people who have a brain aneurysm die on the spot; of the remaining, one half die in the hospital prior to an operation; of those remaining, one half die on the operating table. After hearing the dismal statistics, I called Gutterman's Funeral Parlor on Long Island to make arrangements. It was then that I realized that we would be leaving her burial place to the discretion of the people at the funeral home. We were faced with the prospect that my 50-year old wife would never see her children again and that we might never again see her beaming smile. I called my doctor on Long Island to find out what kind of a hospital Albany Medical Center was, he told me that she couldn't be at a better facility for dealing with a brain aneurysm.

My brother Vic drove down that evening in the pouring rain; Rose, Anne, Mae and Sal followed the next day. Seeing them helped calm me and my son Steve quite a bit. We were allowed to stay with her day and night; she finally woke up after four days, weak but lucid. The bleeding had stopped as the blood around the wound coagulated. She was given a choice by the doctors; she could go home and hope that the wound would remain closed, or she could undergo an operation and put a clip on the artery that ballooned and burst. They impressed on her that going home would be risky, the same as carrying a time bomb around, but then again, they said, she might not have another incident. Barbara made the hard choice of having the operation, which did have a degree of risk, but it was her choice, and she made it wisely. They had to wait for her to build up some strength, so it was a few days before they operated. After the procedure, she was back in a semi-coma for a few days. We thought we had lost her again, but the doctors assured us that she would be okay. We all took one hour turns in holding Barbara's hand and talking to her, it was my sister Mae who hit the jackpot. Barbara woke to see my sister's beautiful smiling face, we were ecstatic when she said, "Where am I?" Well to make a long story short, after 22-days in the hospital, we took her home where she could recover under our watchful eyes and the special care of her parents. As soon as things settled down, I began hunting for a burial plot for the family; going through the same experience of uncertainty and not knowing where we would be buried when the time came, was unsettling to my family. I found a nonsectarian cemetery in East

Moriches, Long Island and purchased ten plots where my brother Vic and his wife Rose; my sister Mae and husband Sal; my sister Anne and Barbara and myself would have a final resting place. I had my parents disinterred from their burial ground in Brooklyn and buried them in our family plot on Long Island. Unfortunately the plots are filling quickly. First my brother-in-law Sal passed away; a month later my sister Mae joined him, and some years later my dear guardian-sister Anne filled her designated spot.

How did providence come into play in this scenario? Steve chose the right location to go to college; it was near one of the most renowned hospitals in the country for aneurysm procedures, with some of the best doctors in that field, Dr. A. John Popp, Chairman of the Neurology Department, in particular. Providence put Barbara in harm's way, and then provided the means for her recovery. We have often discussed what would have happened to both of us if Barbara was driving back, as planned, and she would have had a seizure while holding the wheel of the car. The experience was certainly a wake-up call; we both started looking at life quite differently from that time on, realizing that a long future was most certainly not guaranteed.

Providence again played a role in our lives, this time it was my turn. My dear friend, Chuck Kaufman, age 47, was one of our head salesmen at Manchester Technologies, and my partner's brother-in-law. While having breakfast one morning, he keeled over and died on the spot from a heart attack. He was the youngest of our executives, so after the funeral, we arranged for all of the corporate officers to visit a cardiologist for thorough examinations, including stress-tests. We made appointments for 12 people, including me and my partners. Everyone passed the stress-test except me. The doctor stopped in the middle of the test and said I was having a problem. Of course I immediately went into denial; I was in good physical condition, didn't smoke, had a positive attitude and felt pretty good. So I ignored the doctor's suggestion to have an angiogram to determine what kind of blockage, if any, my arteries had. After about two weeks of nagging from the doctor and Barbara, I agreed to have my arteries explored. I went to St. John's Hospital in Smithtown and had the procedure done. Thanks to the valium that I ingested, and the experienced doctors who performed the intrusion into my body, the whole process went well and is still only a vague memory to me. Well, they found two main arteries almost completely blocked. While still under the influence of the valium, they transported me by ambulance from Smithtown, which is in the eastern part of Long Island, to St. Luke's Hospital in Manhattan, which was a two hour ride with sirens blaring and cars parting to let us pass. The next day I was on the operating table having my chest sawed open so they could hook me up to an artificial heart-lung machine. The next step was to remove my heart and attach two of my chest's mammary arteries to it, thereby bypassing the clogged ones. Well thank God for valium and other mind blocking medications, the whole procedure, which took four-hours, was dreamlike and I didn't feel a thing, that is until I awoke two-days later; I looked like the back of a computer, with tubes sticking out of me and traveling in every imaginable direction. After a ten day stay at the hospital, I returned home a different person physically and mentally. I lost so much weight that looking in the mirror was a frightening experience. Mentally I was in a state of shock, and couldn't believe that my body had failed me so dismally. It was a feeling of betrayal, I relied on my body to take care of itself, and it failed to do so.

At age 57, the experience was not a turning point in my life, but was certainly a wake-up-call that made me the gym fanatic that I am today. It added a dimension to my life that was previously missing by recognizing that "Healthy people do healthy things." So away with eating fatty foods, no more red meats and adhering to a vegetarian diet four days a week, which became our eating lifestyles. My wonderful wife Barbara went on the same diet to make sure I behaved myself and ate what was considered a somewhat fat free diet. Due to our near-death experiences, I decided that it was time for me to start thinking about retiring. It took two years to accomplish that feat, which was certainly a major turning point; at age 59, I was no longer fully employed. My partners insisted that I sign a three year contract and work 52-days a year. This fit in very well with my plans, as we had an office in Boca Raton, Florida, where Barbara and I could spend our winter months in the sunshine; she basking in the sun and me on the golf course. In the summer months I worked at our Hauppauge, Long Island office, in our spare time Barbara and I could be found on our 42-foot Chris Craft, Mikara, traveling throughout the beautiful islands of Cape Code, Rhode Island, and Long Island, which I wrote about in detail in my book "Dancing Around the World With Mike and Barbara Bivona."

Our love of boating brought us from an 18-foot Crestliner runabout, "Big One," which we kept at Passquarella's Marina in Bergen Beach, Brooklyn, where my father-in-law Charley kept his 28-foot makeshift boat by the name of "No Yak" (No Talking); to a 28-foot Chris Craft, "Alice 'B'," that we docked on the South Shore of Long Island at Nick's Marina next to the Shinnecock Inlet, and at Stirling Harbor Marina in Greenport on the North Shore of Long Island; to a 35-foot Chris Craft, and finally a 42-foot Chris Craft, both docked at Stirling Harbor Marina. We have been at that marina for over 35-years and love the summer life that we have, enjoying boating, and traveling when the occasion suits our fancy. It's difficult to explain the passion that sailors have for their boats and their love of sea air. We loved it so much that in 1992 we started the "Stirling Harbor Yacht Club." I wrote the "By Laws" for the club which incorporated parts from the United States Power Squadron's "By Laws" and other yacht clubs' sections to develop what we considered a unique set of rules. The main difference from other clubs is that there is no voting for officers' positions, except in the first year of the organization; all officers move up in rank until they become Commodores. The Commodore chooses his Fleet Captain, who eventually rises in rank from Rear Commodore, Vice Commodore, and finally Commodore. The Board of Directors are chosen by using a "Hat Picking" procedure. Those wishing to serve on the board put their names in a hat, and if lucky are chosen to serve for two years. My objective was to remove politics from the club by eliminating voting for officers and board members. The opening paragraph of our "By Laws" states: "Its purpose is to support yachting, boating, and the associated activities that it encompasses, and to encourage good seamanship and fellowship through racing, cruising, social and educational activities, and to act as a liaison, as appropriate, between its membership, Stirling Harbor

Marina and other boating clubs." The first Commodore was my friend and fellow founder, Herb Kramer, I was the second Commodore and I'm proud to report that the club will be celebrating its 20th anniversary in 2012. We have traveled as a club to Montauk Point, Long Island; Block Island, Rhode Island; Martha's Vineyard, Nantucket, Hyannis, Falmouth and Provincetown, Massachusetts; various parts of Main; Newport, Rhode Island; Mystic, Essex, Clinton, and East Norwich, Connecticut. A copy of our cover of the annual club's directory follows:

YACHT CLUB

2008

The lettering is blue, the Bug Lighthouse, which is located in Orient, N.Y., is white, and the light beam is yellow.

During that time there were two major adjustments to the lives of our immediate family. My brother-in-law Sal Curti died at the age of 67, and in a little over a month, at the age of 64, my sweet sister Mae also passed away. Our family was a close knit group. We would traditionally spend every Easter and Christmas Eve at Mae and Sal's house with our children, my sister Anne and Barbara's parents. They would spend every Thanksgiving and Christmas Day at our house with their children and grandchildren, joining my sister Anne and several of our friends. For many years in February we would have an "Italian Day" at my home where Mae, Sal, Anne, Vic and Rose would spend the day with us enjoying the lasagna that I cooked, under strict supervision from Barbara. We all would wear an Italian symbolic shirt, hat, apron or other ornament while we sang and played toy instruments from our music collection that we accumulated from around the world. Among them were castanets from Greece, wooden clappers from Sicily, tiny drums from Spain, a mouth organ from Argentina and a kazoo from the U.S.

They were the first deaths in our family in a very long time and shocked all of us to the core. The religious holidays that we celebrated with them for over 20-years, came to an abrupt end, changing forever our holiday spirit. The two people who were so instrumental in our lives became a footnote in our prayers at the holiday dinner table. We also lost my best boating and fishing buddy, Barbara's father Charlie Selden at age 84, and in 2003 Barbara's mother Frances, age 91, was also taken from us. We still celebrated our traditional Thanksgiving and Christmas holidays at our home on Broadley Court, but the faces around the dinner table no longer had life's battle marks on their faces, they were the faces of our shiny and bright eyed children, grandchildren, my sister Anne and some close friends. In 2005 my sister-guardian Anne also was not present at our holiday table; she passed away at age 78, leaving my brother Vic, sister Rose, my wife Barbara and me as the remaining members of our once large close knit family.

Two major events in our lives concerned the marriage of our children Steve and Laurie. As we buried members of our family we were fortunate to also add to our number. The new members didn't change the direction that our lives were traveling, but it did enhance the quality of our lives and filled the gaps that were made upon the deaths of our dear family members. The first new addition to our family was Donna Conrad from Mineola, Long Island. She and Steve were married in 1995 at the Swan Club overlooking Roslyn Harbor in the Town of Roslyn. The club's brochure described the feeling we had that day while attending the wedding ceremony and reception. "The Swan Club is a photographer's paradise with background settings so complete that your wedding album will bristle with excitement. The bride's walk… wishing well bridge…gazebo…waterfall…and dancing water fountains will enhance your photographic memories. The lush landscaped gardens on seven acres are constantly maintained with seasonal flower changes. Your guests will marvel at the beauty surrounding them." That is what we expected when we arrived on that August day, but providence had other plans. After not raining for over a month, the morning began with a downpour and didn't let up until near the end of the reception. All the beautiful outdoor scenery could only be enjoyed through the large bay windows from inside the hall. But there is an old farmer's saying, "If it rains on your wedding day it is an omen that your marriage will be blessed with many fine crops." Well, it turned out to be a fruitful marriage blessed with two fine crops, Ian Charles, who was born in Hawaii in 1999 and Catie who was born in Virginia in 2003.

Laurie Jo Bivona brought another new member to our family when she married Clint Gharib a resident of Atlanta, Georgia. They were married in 2006 at the Ritz-Carlton Resort, Rose Hall, on the island of Jamaica. Laurie had always dreamed of having a beachside wedding with the sound of the surf harmonizing with the preacher's blessings. That is what she wanted, and that is what she got. The hotel's brochure described perfectly the setting of the ceremony and reception; "Sequester yourself on a secluded white sand beach, with shimmering waters and lush green mountains rising in the background. Unwind to the rhythmic sounds of Reggae and trust your palate to authentic Caribbean flavors. Glide along rivers in the island's lush interior or swim with horses in the ocean spray." The wedding gave us an opportunity to meet Clint's family and to spend time with him and his beautiful sister Lydia and her children and his wonderful mother Sharon. Clint's father Jim, an avid golfer, wanted to play the challenging golf course on the island, but the weather wouldn't cooperate, good thing, I had a 22 handicap, he later told me that his was 2, what a massacre that would have been. Their wedding day was also sprinkled with blessings as it rained on and throughout the ceremony and reception. The happy occasion didn't change the direction that Barbara and I were traveling, but it broadened and enhanced the quality of our lives by having another son in the family.

The end of my employment contract coincided with Manchester Technologies becoming a public company trading on the stock exchange (NASDAQ), its symbol was MEC. The small company that I first joined 11-years ago had become a conglomerate with hundreds of employees and offices in several major cities. Barbara and I had traveled the long road from marriage, to raising a family, running a business, and my finally becoming a captain of industry. We were then faced with retiring, which was a major turning point for both Barbara and me. We asked ourselves, what exactly does retiring mean? Do we buy rocking chairs and pass the time of day doing crossword puzzles and playing checkers? Do we start making plans for entering a nursing home? Do we start looking for new hobbies to occupy our time? Was it time to permanently settle in Florida? Well the one thing we knew for sure was that if we spent entire days together, we would probably both end up in insane asylums. So my first step was to leave Barbara as the queen of her domain on Broadley Court and for me to rent an office in Deer Park to maintain my business holdings and to finish writing my book "Business Infrastructure in a Computer Environment." Having my own office also allowed me to indulge in one of my favorite pastimes, reading history books, especially those covering Christopher Columbus and the age of discovery, from years 1,400 to 1,700. I already had an extensive book collection on the subject and spending my spare time adding to my library and catching up on reading became a passion for me. I was also a chartered member of the congressional designated "Christopher Columbus 500 Quincentenary

Jubilee Commission," and the New York "Countdown 1992" organization that promoted the Expo 92 world event.

Barbara and I went to Seville, Spain for two weeks to take part in the World's Fair-Expo '92, "Columbus and the age of Discovery," as spectators for the New York organization "Countdown 1992." The Expo was from April 20 to October 12, 1992, on La Isla de La Cartuja, in Seville. Over 100 countries were represented, they were spread out over 500 acres. We were there for several days, including the finale on October 12, and became part of the history of that event, which recorded over 41-million visitors. A poster of the 1992 Seville-Expo '92 follows:

Continuing my education of the age of discovery was not only a learning experience but became an obsession for collecting additional books and gathering enough information to one day possibly writing a book about that era. Years later I would donate over 300 of my books that took over 30-years to collect, to the Columbus Foundation. The organization is the sponsor of the annual Columbus Day Parade in New York City, of which I was a special guest for the year of the donation. My collection now resides in their extensive library, which had only a sprinkling of books on the subject at the time of my contribution. A copy of the Foundation's newsletter mentioning my donation follows as well as a picture of the library that was set aside for the:

Michael Bivona Collection:

Columbus, the Age of Discovery and Related Books

Donated, March 2006

Bivona Collection Donated

The Foundation has received an enormously generous and essential donation, the Michael Bivona Collection: Columbus, The Age of Discovery and Related Books. The collection, which Mr. Bivona acquired over the course of 30 years, contains approximately 300 books and immediately gives us an extensive group of works about the Foundation's namesake. It will reside in the Ambassador Charles A. Gargano Library.

"This remarkable donation, by Michael Bivona, vastly increases and improves the quality of our library's holdings," said President Louis Tallarini. " We are deeply grateful to Mr. Bivona for his donation, and we are proud that our Member Louis Mangone made the introduction that has brought the Michael Bivona Collection to the Foundation."

"The age of discovery was roughly 1400 to 1700, and of course Columbus was central to the period," said Mr. Bivona. "He had the audacity and the courage to venture out into unknown areas. At that time, very few people would venture out on the water beyond the sight of land. He had few navigational instruments to guide him when he became the first European to discover and record this unknown continent. He found his way back to Spain using his knowledge of celestial navigation, ocean currents and prevailing winds. The route he took is still being used today because of the favorable winds and currents. What he did was just amazing."

Mr. Bivona, 72, and his wife Barbara live in Dix Hills, Long Island and have two grown children and two grandchildren. Now retired, he was a CPA and co-owner and CFO of Manchester Technologies. His main hobbies are boating and ballroom dancing. He owns a 42-foot Cris-Craft boat, which they've taken to Block Island, Cape Cod, Nantucket and Plymouth, among other places, but, unlike Columbus, he said, "with very sophisticated electronic navigational devices."

Foundation News

Mr. Bivona and Foundation Member Louis Mangone belong to a dancing group that meets regularly. Several months ago, Mr. Bivona was in discussions with Brown University, in Providence, Rhode Island, about donating the collection to the school. "I mentioned to Lou Mangone that I was talking to Brown, and he told me that the Foundation would be interested in the collection." Mr. Mangone pursued the collection, which is now coming to the Foundation.

Book collector, philanthropist and ballroom dance aficionado Michael Bivona with wife Barbara in a tango

The Michael Bivona Collection has great depth in its holdings of books about Columbus, from his own letters and journals and contemporary accounts of his voyages to the works of later historians who interpret and comment on the lasting changes brought about by his explorations. Mr. Bivona acquired the books from every type of source imaginable, from specialized booksellers to bookstores and flea markets, and the books range in age from recent to over 100 years old.

"It is wonderful to know that my collection will have a meaningful place at the Foundation to honor a great explorer," Mr. Bivona said. ❖

Providence was instrumental in my having the opportunity to place my collection at the prestigious organization. We were at Dan Maloney's Empress Ballroom in Delray Beach, Florida enjoying our usual Friday night social dance party, when I was introduced to Lou Mangone who was a member of the Columbus Foundation and in charge of their library. I mentioned that I was in negotiation with Brown University, in Providence, Rhode Island about donating some of my collection to their Americana Collection of books on the age of discovery. I was a long standing member of the Brown University Library and was excited that they were considering adding some of my books to their world renowned Americana Collection. Lou said his organization would be very interested in my books and could probably keep them as a collection in a separate area of their library. The prospect of having the collection stay intact under my name was very compelling; Brown University would have scattered the books in their respective categories throughout their humongous library, which meant that I would lose the recognition of the collection. So to make a long story short, I indexed my collection and shipped them off to the foundation, where they reside today for the pleasure of their members and researchers.

Barbara and I dreamed that when we retired, we would be spending as much time on our 42-foot Chris Craft cruiser as possible and even taking her from New York on an extended trip to Florida. The first summer of our retirement we took a month long trip that included stopping at Montauk Point, Long Island; Block Island, Rhode Island; Martha's Vineyard and Nantucket, Massachusetts; Hyannis and Falmouth, in Cape Cod, Massachusetts; New Bedford in Buzzard's Bay, Massachusetts, and our last stop away from home, Newport, Rhode Island. By the time we ended our voyage we were on the verge of going stir-crazy. Our dream of spending endless days aboard Mikara became a reality, but the reality didn't match our dreams. When employed it was a necessity and great fun to have a boat as an escape from life's daily pressures, but if there is no stress to escape from then a boat becomes another responsibility. We researched taking Mikara to Florida in the winter months. When we calculated the cost of the fuel, the overnight dockage along the way, and the possibility of repairs, the estimate was just too expensive, and we quickly changed our minds. So we had to find other things to occupy our time during retirement.

The Salvation Army was preparing a facility for homeless veterans at the East Northport Veterans Hospital which is located on the North Shore of Long Island. I became one of their advisors for establishing temporary living quarters on the hospital grounds for homeless veterans. It took several years of hard work to get proper bedding, furnishing and cooking facilities in place, but eventually we got the program running pretty smoothly, and today it's one of the few homeless facilities on eastern Long Island where clients can stay and hopefully recuperate from their unfortunate circumstances. In addition I became active in the "Children of Hope" program in Deer Park. The essence of the program was to feed people in need and to support and guide children in the Wyandanch area who needed physical and mental support. Raising funds to provide food for the clients was a major endeavor and the volunteers worked 24/7 on behalf of the recipients. The program is still in operation today and is an essential part of the Deer Park and Wyandanch communities.

In addition to my busy charitable schedule, I was instrumental in the opening of the state-of-the-art "Michael Bivona Graduate Student Center" at the C.W. Post Campus of Long Island University, located in Brookville, Long Island. A copy of the dedication news release is below:

Getting You From Where You Are . . . To Where You Want To Be

C.W. POST CAMPUS

Office of Public Relations | What's New

<-- Go Back...

Bivona Graduate Student Center Dedication

On December 4, 2002, C.W. Post celebrated the dedication of the new Bivona Graduate Student Center in Roth Hall. Benefactors Michael and Barbara Bivona were joined by members of administration, students and faculty of the College of Management at the celebration.

Joseph Shenker, Provost of the C.W. Post Campus, Long Island University alum Michael Bivona, and Robert Sanator, Dean of the C.W. Post College of Management

Michael Bivona with wife Barbara at the dedication of The Michael Bivona Graduate Student Center

The Bivona Graduate Student Center will serve as headquarters for the College of Management's AACSB-accredited Master of Business Administration program and as a study area for the College's graduate students. The center, which opened on August 29, brings together all the resources of the MBA program, including academic advising, and provides a place for students to work together, conduct research, consult with advisors and meet with faculty. It features work areas with tables, desks, computers with Internet connections, laptop ports, printers and copiers as well as staff and advisors' offices.

Donor Michael Bivona, a certified public accountant and retired chief financial officer of Manchester Technologies, Inc., graduated from Long Island University's Brooklyn Campus in 1960 with a B.S. in business.

Graduate students at C.W. Post enjoying the dedication of The Michael Bivona Graduate Student Center

Phone: 516-299-2333 | Email pr@cwpost.liu.edu

Long Island University   C.W. Post Campus

Barbara and I also became founders of the "Tilles Center for the Performing Arts" reconstruction program, at the C.W. Post Campus. The program brought the venue into the 21st Century technologically, with excellent seating, stage, acoustical and visual aides for the comfort of the audience and performers.

Due to my four years in the Air Force and Jet Set experiences, I remained an avid flyboy, and couldn't resist assisting in the development of the "Cradle of Aviation Museum" which is located in Garden City, Long Island, at my former home on the Mitchel Air Force Base site. What made the effort interesting was that the museum was to be built where I spent the last year of my enlistment in the Air Force. The museum now is an aerospace museum and was built to commemorate Long Island's part in the history of aviation. Mitchel AFB together with nearby Roosevelt Field and other airfields on the Hempstead Plains were the sites of many historic flights, which gave the area as early as the 1920s the name of the "Cradle of Aviation." Some of the memorable flights from the plains were the first attempted Atlantic crossing in a balloon in 1873, which lasted only four hours and ended up in Connecticut a dismal failure, to the more successful flight of Charles Lindbergh in 1927 from Mitchel Field to Paris, France in the first nonstop fixed-winged aircraft, covering 3,600 miles and taking 33 hours. It was the first flight of its kind from the United States to Europe and opened the door to what today is an everyday flying experience.

Mitchel AFB was purchased by Nassau County in the early 1960s. It wasn't until the early 1980s that the museum opened with a handful of aircraft housed in the old hangers that were a part of the AFB base when I was stationed there. Some of the aircraft that were being restored by the many volunteers who were retirees from Grumman and Republic Aviation were: Charles Lindbergh's first Curtiss Jenny, the Ryan Brougham (sister ship of the Spirit of St. Louis); Republic's P-47N Thunderbolt, Republic's Seabee, Grumman's F-11A Tiger, and a Grumman Lunar Module spacecraft. These aircraft are now housed in hangars 3 & 4 of the old Mitchel AFB.

It was in the early 1980s that I became active and fascinated with the dream of having a world-class aviation museum on Long Island. I immediately became a member of the organization and pledged to provide the funds to create a replica of the "Lilienthal Glider." It was built for display in the first exhibit, the "Dream of Flight" of the museum which opened in 2002, as a state-of-the-art facility. Today the museum contains over 60 aircraft and scale models of airplanes from various time periods. Some interesting exhibits are an actual unused Apollo Lunar Space Module, my Lilienthal Glider, an A-10 Thunderbolt II, a Grumman F-14 Tomcat, and even a Russian Sputnik, which was donated by that country, and is the sister ship of the original that was the first spacecraft to orbit the earth in the late 1950s. The facility also has an IMAX theater and the most pleasant and knowledgeable volunteer guides, many of whom are former employees of Grumman and Republic, waiting to assist visitors and to answer questions. The Lilienthal Glider was built in 1891 by Otto Lilienthal of Germany. He hoped to demonstrate the possibility of "Flight by man." Their replica is of his 1894 glider which was considered the most successful of his designs. The movement of the pilot's body, suspended between the wings, altered the machine's center of gravity and provided a marginally effective control. Flying it off a high hill, he made many flights before suffering a fatal crash in 1896. He demonstrated that air could support a man in winged flight. His influence on aeronautical progress in the world was tremendous, and therefore, the glider on display is a tribute to an imaginative scientist who gave his life in the development of his dream, which he knew one day would become a reality. The Exhibits at the museum are:

Dream of Wings, 1870-1903

The Hempstead Plains, 1904-1913

World War I, 1914-1918

The Golden Age, 1919-1939

World War II, 1940-1945

The Jet Age, 1946-1995

Aviation Today 1995—

A copy of a Lilienthal Glider replica follows:

We used to visit Barbara's parents in Florida often. Her father Charley died in 1991 at age 84. He was my mentor in boat repairs and also my boating and fishing buddy. We spent many a lazy-day fishing in New York and Florida, I miss him dearly. Her mother passed away in 2003 at age 91 after a long bedridden illness. Their deaths were not turning points in our lives, but a major change in our life-styles. Our visits to Florida were always focused on visiting Barbara's parents to make sure they were living comfortably and had all that was necessary to do so. If we had time, we would squeeze mini-vacations in where possible while visiting them. We decided that the time was right to spend extended quality time in sunny-Disneyland, so we bought a home-away-from-home in Delray Beach-Boca Raton, at the Polo Club. The three entrances to the club are all in Boca Raton, but we live across the C15 Canal that separates the two towns within our complex, and therefore our address is in Delray, Beach. We currently spend six winter months in Florida and six summer months in New York.

One of the main problems that I have with retirement is that there are too many things happening and not enough time to appreciate them all. Choosing what to do becomes confusing and very stressful, and many times creates conflicts in scheduling and entertainment. I found myself going to the gym three times a week; dancing two to three times a week; taking dancing lessons at least once a week; writing my second and third books; boating in the summer in New York; playing golf in Florida in the winter and in New York in the summer, and traveling around the world whenever we could. All of these activities made my life more stressful than when I was employed. So I made a priority list. The gym was a necessity, dictated by my open-heart-bypass-surgery, that I had to continue to stay healthy and in good physical condition; I also enjoyed the work outs. Boating was a part of our lives since we first got married over 45-years ago, it was something we loved doing and couldn't think of giving up. Dancing had become a part of our very souls, so giving up something we loved and were good at was also out of the question. Writing in my senior years became something that I felt compelled to do, I don't know why, but it seems I can't stay away from the keyboard, (it might have something to do with my beautiful typing teacher in junior high school). That left golf. I was taking lessons at least once a week, and playing twice a week. Regardless of the lessons and the perceived progress that I was making, I really stunk at the game. My handicap was 22 on a good day, and I couldn't get it any lower. So the most logical stressor for me to eliminate, was golf, which I did three years ago, and now I have just the right amount of time to indulge in my other passions; as a bonus I no long have the constant feeling that I should be better than I am by improving my useless golf game.

The zenith of my life is readily described in the "2007 Distinguished Alumni Award" I received in May of 2007 from Long Island University at their Brooklyn Campus, which is given to two alumni a year. Donning my academic mortarboard and gown for the second time in my life, was in sharp contrast to my first wearing it at the same university 47-years prior.

The first occasion was the beginning of the first door opening on my trip into the unknown. The second time was the conclusion of my journey and the accolade that was bestowed on me by my fellow peers for what they concluded was a job well done. What more can a person ask for? A copy of the presentation of the award follows:

DISTINGUISHED ALUMNI AWARDS

MICHAEL BIVONA '60
Retired, Part Owner, C.F.O., C.O.O., Manchester Technologies, Inc.

Born and raised in the East New York section of Brooklyn, Michael Bivona dropped out of school at the age of 16 and joined the United States Air Force in 1952. He obtained his G.E.D. and served as a communications specialist in Japan before completing his service in 1956.

Once home, Mr. Bivona excelled personally and professionally, immersing himself in accounting studies at Long Island University's Brooklyn Campus. He became president of the Accounting Society and the Veteran's Club and worked in the accounting department. He was granted a CPA license following his graduation with a bachelor of science in 1960.

After a number of years in private practice, he expanded his accounting firm, partnering with C.W. Post alumnus, Louis M. Ambrico '73. He next invested in Manchester Technologies, Inc., becoming part owner, C.F.O. and C.O.O. His combined expertise in the areas of technology and finance helped to fuel the computer supplier's rapid growth by the time the company went public in 1996.

Today, Mr. Bivona and his wife, Barbara, devote their time and financial resources to a broad array of philanthropic causes. They are generous supporters of Long Island University. Mrs. Bivona is a member of the Tilles Center board of overseers. Mr. Bivona funded the C.W. Post Bivona Graduate Student Center and is an executive member of the College of Management board of advisors. Mr. Bivona also recently donated the 300-volume "Michael Bivona Collection: Columbus, the Age of Discovery and Related Books," to the Columbus Citizens Foundation, an organization dedicated to preserving Italian-American heritage.

A man of diverse interests and talents, Mr. Bivona is the author of "Business Infrastructure in a Computer Environment," which was published by Vantage Press in 2001. He is an avid boater and a ballroom dancing aficionado who loves to perform with his wife.

The Bivonas live in Dix Hills, Long Island and have two children and two grandchildren.

Well, the above article about sums up my life. Barbara and I are now coasting along enjoying our golden years visiting with our children, Steve and Donna and Laurie and Clint, and of course, our grandchildren Ian and Catie. The highlights of our current lives are dancing and traveling. We are members of USA DanceSport and honorary members of Argentine Tango Lovers of Long Island.

We can usually be found at the various dance venues that we attend at least two or three times a week. We also give Argentine Tango exhibitions at various dance halls and social occasions. As the dance has become very popular, many of our friends have asked us to give them lessons, which we gladly do at their homes and at the dance halls we attend. To round out our dancing experience, we are still taking lessons once a week from Brian Smith in Pompano Beach, Florida, and Louis Del Prete, in Long Island. Our passion for traveling is still alive and well. In 2009 we flew to London, England for four days visiting the Tower of London, Buckingham Palace, Westminster Abbey, Big Ben, Tower of London, The Eye (which is a Ferris wheel that overlooks London), the Aquarium, and of course Harrods Department Store. From there we took the ship, "Jewel of the Seas," a 5,000 passenger liner, to the Baltic Sea Countries of Norway, Denmark, Finland, Sweden, Estonia and St. Petersburg, Russia. This year we are traveling by plane to Phoenix , Arizona and staying in the beautiful city of Scottsdale for a couple of days and then moving on to, Sedona, the National Grand Canyon, Lake Powell, the Hoover Dam, Bryce Canyon, Zion Canyon, and Las Vegas, where we will be spend three days resting from the arduous journey. While staying at Caesar's Palace we plan to visit the Liberace Museum, and the Venetian Resort, where we will go on a Gondola ride, and then sample some of their fine Italian cuisine. . . .